THE THRILLS OF A START-UP

CORPORATE STORIES OF FIVE DECADES

UTPAL K DUTTA

Copyright © 2024 Utpal K Dutta

All Rights Reserved.

No part of this book may be reproduced, or stored in a retrieval system, or transmitted in any form or by any means, electronic, mechanical, photocopying, recording, or otherwise, without the express written permission of the author.

This book is a memoir. It reflects the author's present recollections of experiences over time. Some names and characters have been changed, some events have been compressed, and some dialogue has been recreated based on author's memory.

First Edition: May 2024

Cover By: Lalit & Prashantt - Story Mirror

Published By: Moyna Books
www.moynabooks.com

ISBN -10: 0998016713

ISBN -13: 978-0-9980167-1-9

TESTIMONIAL 1

"Sankalp Shuddha hi Siddha" (meaning noble desire brings success) is what my Guru Maharaj ji taught me as my lesson in life. Paulo Coelho said something similar in his book The Alchemist - "When you want something, all the universe conspires to help you achieve it." The author, Dr Dutta is a living example of how he has succeeded in life through various avatar with a single minded, clear and dedicated goal, "**Shuddha** Sankalpa."

Graduate from IIT Kharagpur, PhD from United Kingdom in the 1960s, goes to speak a lot about the academic capabilities of the person. Most of the people of that generation in India with academic credentials, headed for the Civil Service or the Engineering Services cadre of the government, landing up doing more administrative jobs than technical. Dr Dutta chose his passion to continue discovering new things all his life and setting up a roadmap for people to follow. He aptly calls these the start-ups. In a subtle way he has also expressed that he was a free bird and always chose "what to do."

With his noble and ambitious dreams, he pursued a thrilling corporate life, which he has documented in the book in his lucid style of storytelling. The narrative, interspersed with anecdotes and snippets, never gives a dull moment. The stories turn out to be lessons in management. Two of his expressions have touched me deeply. One is "always asking yourself when is the last time you did something for the first time" and the other his spirit of enjoying the sheer joy "of doing nothing."

Prof (Dr.) Arup Roy Choudhury
Fellow Institution of Engineers
Lead Assessor, IQA (U.K.)
M. Tech & Ph.D. IIT-Delhi
BSc. Engineering (Hons) Civil Engineering BIT Mesra
Formerly:
Professor, DMS IIT Delhi
Principal Advisor Infra to GoWB,
Chief Commissioner, WBRTPS, GoWB
Chairman and Managing Director, NTPC & NBCC
Founder Chairman NTPC School of Business

TESTIMONIAL 2

The Author, Dr. Dutta left a secure and prospective position in a major engineering company to enjoy the thrills of a series of start-ups, on invitation from lesser-known small companies. And he succeeded in it, starting from a scratch.

All that gave him a unique experience of working in a place full of thousands of engineers and then sitting alone in a start-up company to create something big. He shares the remarkable experience of five decades of his corporate life and corporate adventures, through real-life stories and snippets, which make the book very engrossing to read.

The author's story telling style is simple and down to earth. Even in the chapters on a major start-up, he tells us about strategies adopted, mistakes and successes in the journey along the uncertain path, through anecdotes and snippets.

On the whole, the book comes out as life's lessons in human interactions and management.

Rajiv Mehrotra
Global Business Developer and Technopreneur
Singapore

TESTIMONIAL 3

Those were the days when the term "Start-up" was not familiar in India. Technology-rich and strategic businesses were conceived only by the Public Sector and that too in collaboration with established multinationals. Even large business conglomerates hesitated to enter.

That was when Dr Dutta, having left his position with a bright future in Engineers India Ltd, grabbed an offer to start-up an Indian engineering consultancy organization to cater to the Oil & Gas industry, a field mainly controlled by multinationals. He played the key role in building it up to international standards of quality, professionalism and size.

But the EPC company he established was not his only start-up effort. Dr Dutta has been a "serial" start-up professional. Whenever the start-up venture got established, he felt stifled and cocooned, and flew out to establish another one!

In the process, he gained expertise and knowledge and encountered worlds of varied culture. Dr Dutta shares these experiences, along with management insights, in a delightful story-form, sprinkling it with anecdotes, giving the narration a smooth flow, making the book eminently readable.

R. Jaishankar
Ex-President SNC Lavalin Engineering India P. Ltd.
Founder and Ex-Managing Director
RJ Associates (Engineers) P. Ltd.
(Later Acquired by SNC Lavalin,
a major EPC Company of Canada)

Dedication

To people with whom I came into contact
From the day I was born till now
Who made life so interesting
Parents, wife, siblings, extended families
Children and their families
Close ones, corporate colleagues, friends
Specially remembering those who are no more
Thank you all.

ACKNOWLEDGEMENTS

Writing the book recalling incidents in my professional life was an intense experience and took time. It was possible due to the support, contribution and encouragement of many. I would like to specially acknowledge the effort and contribution of -

Robin Sarkar, who is doctorate in management and held top management positions in major US organizations, for his review and valuable suggestions.

Rajiv Mehrotra, a global business developer and technopreneur based in Singapore, for review of the manuscript, valuable comments and suggestions.

Deepali Dutta for her encouragement and patient editing as I kept the churning on by redoing and revising parts of the manuscript often.

To Rini Dutta, Arup Dutta and Varun Natarajan for valuable comments and inputs.

Cogs in The Wheel

In my book, the main characters are those who play a pivotal role in shaping the companies. I wish to express my heartfelt gratitude to those who serve from behind the scenes as the essential backbone, propelling operations forward with their unwavering dedication and hard work. Besides technical professionals, they include HRD & administrative personnel, secretaries, finance personnel and others. Their invaluable support has been indispensable in moving forward the wheels in the organizations I worked with.

CONTENTS

The Curtain Raiser   1
A backdrop on five decades of my corporate journey.

1. Good to Great   5
Life and times in a company that gave me the experience, capability and confidence to embark on later adventures.

2. A Trial by Fire   31
Transition from hustle bustle of a big company to start a business of an American company, all alone in a single room office.

3. The Thrills of a Start-up   49
Charting a new path, an unknown, untrodden path, with surprises and adventure.

4. Breaking Barriers in Singapore   101
The thrills of a win in an international arena.

5. Freedom! Freedom!   125
Freedom to do what I love to do and not do what I do not love to do.

Afterword   139
Miles to go before I sleep.

THE CURTAIN RAISER

Does *destiny* set your future? Or is it *hard work*? Or *luck*?

Gaur Gopal Das, a well-known motivational speaker in India, nicely defined the difference between them. Destiny is a situation that comes to you on which you have no choice. For example, your birth – you don't choose who will be your parents. That is your destiny.

But situations occur in life where you have a 'choice' of response. By choosing the response, you create your own destiny. For example, someone is dissatisfied with his job. He has two choices of response – keep sulking or keep giving his best to the job and try for a change. Which one he chooses sets his destiny.

I was born in a family in India, where educational performance was a tradition. That was a boon from destiny. After completing schooling, I could crack a difficult entrance test to get entry to Indian Institute of Technology in 1958.

That was the first of a chain of premier engineering institutions in India known as IIT, which later became a known brand in US universities and the Silicon Valley.

Which discipline of engineering to choose? My 'choice' was Chemical Engineering, which in the year 1958 was an unknown discipline of engineering in India. The tradition was to go for civil, mechanical or electrical, in that order.

Then why chemical engineering? Perhaps that was a trait in my nature – going for the unknown.

I did my graduation in Chemical Engineering from IIT in 1962 and followed up with a Master's degree. Once I asked my professor what was the opportunity for Chemical Engineers in India. He gave a reply that remained etched in my mind forever.

"In life, you always have to create your own opportunities."

The environment at IIT campus, a 100% residential institution, was unique in shaping the personalities of the students. India is a nation of multiple sub-nationalities and cultures. Travel and communication facilities were poor in India in the 1950's. I had little exposure to different cultures of India. At IIT campus I had the first opportunity to know people, all Indians, who spoke different languages, had a different cuisine and even displayed different mannerisms.

Coming out of IIT, I worked for a couple of years in the petroleum industry. In 1966, I *chose* to leave my job for higher studies and landed in Loughborough University, England. The life in the university in England was my first exposure to a multinational environment. The multicultural exposure at IIT helped me to quickly adapt to it. I started loving it.

During completion of my Ph.D. dissertation in 1969, two job openings cropped up before me. One was with a well-known multinational company in England. Another from a major engineering consultancy company located in New Delhi, India.

Here was again the question of *choice*, a very important one. I chose the India option, though salaries in India were awfully meager those days!

I was six years old when India became independent in 1947, after 200 years of British rule. Ours was a 'joint family' at that time. The cheer and joy in the faces of my parents and a number of loving uncles and aunts all living together, is still vivid in my memory. It was a lasting impression, all about creating a new India, which influenced my choice.

In December 1969, I booked a flight back to New Delhi. On the day of departure, the drive along M4 motorway from London to Heathrow airport put me in a somber mood! England had become like my second home. I felt just as homesick leaving England as I had felt when I left India for studies in England.

With this prelude, let me take you through the five decades of my time travel through the corporate world. It is a journey of an ordinary person, not a high-flying celebrity. But it has been a thrilling journey through the corporate maze, which included one major start-up and a few smaller start-ups. I was often driven by the thought -

"When was the last time you did something for the first time?"

This narrative is in five chapters covering different phases of my corporate life in five organizations. In each of these phases, I had an opportunity to *do something for the first time*.

The journey is told mostly through real life stories and anecdotes, avoiding management or technical jargons. Come, enjoy the time travel with me!

> *"I don't play golf to get second place.
> I either win or gain experience"*
>
> *- Lyle Pedro, a young golf player*

CHAPTER - 1

GOOD TO GREAT

FIRE IN THE BELLY

The title of the chapter is borrowed from a book of the same title by Jim Collins. The book identified the traits and cultures of companies which moved from being good to great companies.

In January, 1970, I returned from England and joined Engineers India Ltd. in New Delhi, often referred as **EIL**. When I joined, it had all the traits and culture of a company moving from being good to a great company.

This was the company that gave me the kind of experience and confidence to venture into startups later.

As I started working on one of the projects, my supervisor Dr. Kochar told me something very inspiring.

"Utpal, we all here are working with *fire in the belly* to achieve a single mission. That mission is to develop complete know-how and capability in India from concept to implementation of complex refinery and petrochemical projects worth several billion dollars."

Very soon I realized that the spirit of the mission of self-reliance had percolated into most of the employees. The salaries were low, but the spirits were soaring high.

But who brought in that spirit?

It was sometime in 1955. One young Indian engineer of that era, M.S. Pathak, a graduate from Massachusetts Institute of Technology (MIT), USA, was working for Caltex, a major petroleum company in the USA. He was working on design and engineering of Caltex Refinery Project in India from their US office.

He was deeply inspired by the call of creating a self-reliant India, from the first Prime Minister of independent India, Nehru.

A question arose in Pathak's mind.

"Why can't we do this in India?" was the question.

"This thought became an obsession with me," he stated later in his memoirs.

India was a closed government-controlled economy those days. Pathak returned to India and relentlessly pushed his vision of creating self-reliance in India with the Government of India. The vision was to create a company with design, engineering and project management capability for mega-projects in oil, natural gas, petroleum refining and other infrastructure projects.

The end result was creation of Engineers India Limited (EIL) sometime in the 1960's, as a joint venture between the government and Bechtel Corporation of USA, a world leader in this kind of business.

With bureaucratic delays in a state-controlled business environment, Bechtel perhaps lost patience after executing some projects and quit. EIL soon became a fully government owned company.

Pathak later became the Chairman and Managing Director.

EIL was fortunate to have already assimilated work culture and project management systems of Bechtel Corporation of USA. The association with Bechtel helped EIL to start on a sound commercial basis, unlike many other state-owned companies.

The organization structure was flat and the communication, both vertical and lateral, was smooth. In any informal gathering of employees, Pathak used to move around and talk freely to everyone.

It was a thriving, multi-disciplinary team of over a thousand engineers when I joined, fired by the mission to create a capability hitherto non-existent in India.

I too got happily immersed in the mission with fire in the belly.

We grew with EIL. EIL grew on us.

*****

TAKING THE BULL BY THE HORN

The power in government held companies was concentrated in the hands of bureaucrats in the government and the finance personnel in the company with their rule books. Pathak took them hands-on to take control.

A Relook at the Way Things Work

A story goes that an engineer made some expenditure without following a long list of procedures and approvals. Someone in the management told him that he should either resign or face action. Pathak called the engineer to hear his side of the story. After analyzing the facts, he issued a notice. It stated –

"The expenditure was done on urgent basis in the interest of expediting a project, resulting in benefit for the company. No action should be taken against the engineer."

Changing the Rule Books

To create such a company, a key element was getting highly skilled professionals, with knowledge base in relevant areas. A smart and eloquent person with missionary passion, Pathak persuaded a number of Indian engineers working in the oil and gas industry in the USA and Europe to return and join EIL. Remember in 1960's, life was hard in India with queue of months to get simple necessities like telephones or cooking gas.

To get them a decent salary, he overturned the rulebooks to pay them salaries much higher than his own! When I joined, EIL had some of the best Indian talents drawn from many parts of the world.

*****

THE LIFE AND TIMES IN EIL

In the environment of teamwork by hundreds working together, the experience in EIL was not only project and technology oriented. The interactions, vertical and lateral, exposed us to some excellent management skills, told here through anecdotes.

Smart Solutions

Chowdhury, Head of our Process Department, was one of the smart managers of people and technically very sound. His background in an operating company, gave him an excellent understanding of how the plant systems work. He used to come out with innovative solutions to design problems as well as management problems.

Once a colleague of mine approached him with a technical issue.

"Don't come to me always with a problem," he smiled at him and replied calmly. "Think, analyze, discuss with your colleagues and come with three possible solutions to the problem. And let me help you choose the best solution. That way both you and I will be most effective."

I recall another smart statement from him where I was the culprit. In EIL salaries were quite low those days. Our greatest attraction was foreign assignments, even if for a short period. We used to get a hefty per day ad hoc allowance with no need to submit any expense report with receipts.

It used to be major source for our savings, besides the fun of a trip abroad.

Once, I was very busy with my team to meet a target on a project report to be submitted in the next few days.

Chowdhury came to me and told me that our director has to deliver a talk on a topic I was familiar with. He asked me to make a few pages of notes for him.

I was neck deep in completing the project report. I requested him to spare me as I was very tight on the schedule.

Then he made a master class statement to me.

"I know you can do it Utpal." He continued, "Suppose I told you that tomorrow evening you have to catch a flight to Houston for an assignment. You would have found ways to do your current job as well as find time to prepare for your overseas assignment. Just imagine that the few hours you will be spending on the paper for our director, as preparation for a foreign assignment. You will not miss the target on what you are doing."

Yes, I did both the tasks, well on time!

The Virtues of Brevity

I was handling some complex problem on transportation of crude oil from Bombay High offshore platforms located in Arabian Sea by undersea pipelines. The oil had tendency to gel easily below 30° C due to high wax content.

Transporting it by pipeline to be laid below the sea, with sea water temperature of 20° C had a potential risk! The 200 kilometer pipeline could get blocked with gelled crude oil!

As a leader of a team of experts responsible for the job, I and my teammates did a thorough study of the problems and possible solutions.

One day Dr. Mitra, one of our directors, called me to his office. He had just returned after a trip to Shell, Holland.

Shell was one of the pioneers in the technology of transportation of waxy and gelling type of crude oils.

He asked me how we were handling the crude oil flow problem. Being quite thorough on the subject, I started off with a longish lecture in great detail.

After five minutes or so, he looked visibly irritated and asked me to stop abruptly. He just handed me a bunch of papers containing the information he brought from Shell on waxy crude and dismissed me in a rather harsh tone!

One of my seniors, Dr. Kochar, an excellent manager, was sitting there and watched the whole scene in silence.

I came back to my room. I was sitting in a slightly depressed mood. Dr. Kochar entered my room and patted my back.

"Don't feel bad Utpal," he said to me, "such things do happen and it is a part of the learning process in interaction. Let me share a similar experience I had when I was your age."

"I was working in Scientific Design Co., in USA those days," he continued. "One day our director popped into my room and asked me to explain some issue. Just like you I started blurting out whatever I knew. He stopped me after a while in an angry mood."

"I don't want to hear a long speech," he told me. "When I ask you a question, you should answer within a few minutes. And you have to find out how to answer me in a few minutes."

Dr. Kochar's story lightened my mood immediately.

Later, as I climbed up in management level, I realized how important this lesson on the virtues of brevity was to me.

I recall another incident while writing this episode. This also happened during my tenure in EIL, while Pathak was still there as the Chairman. Free with people as he was, he entered the project room and asked the Project Manager the reason for delay in a project.

"Sir, I can explain in one minute, in five minutes and in half an hour," the project manager said.

"Which one would you like me to present?" he concluded in a well-humored way.

You Are Also Right!

Two heads of departments had a disagreement over certain project related issues. Both decided to meet the Director (Projects) to sort out the matter. The Director asked each of them to present their viewpoint and logic behind it.

When the first executive finished his presentation, the Director just commented, "Right. You are right from your point of view," and asked the other to present.

When the other executive presented his version, the Director commented, "You are also right."

Both got baffled! How both can be right with opposing views, they wondered.

"Look here," the Director explained. "Many issues in life cannot be seen exactly as white or black. Some are grey, a mix of black and white. Each of you are looking at the issue ignoring the grey areas of your logic."

Then he intervened and resolved the matter!

*****

------------Layman's Guide on EPC Business--------------

Some of my next stories and anecdotes are on achieving the dream of self-reliance. Before that here is a simple explanation of the kind of business executed in the companies where I worked.

Refineries and other oil and gas processing facilities are large, sprawling industrial complexes covering several square kilometers of land. The plant is packed with thousands of pieces of large and complex equipment, interconnected with network of hundreds of kilometers of piping, electrical, optical fibers etc. They have intricate safety and automation systems and control rooms looking like satellite launching stations.

A part of Jamnagar Refinery [Courtesy: Reliance Ind. Ltd.]

Executing such projects requires a team of hundreds or thousands of engineers of all disciplines and specializations. For project execution services, the investing company engages an engineering consultancy company. They provide Knowhow, Design, **E**ngineering, **P**rocurement and **C**onstruction services. They are called **EPC** companies.

It is a **business in providing knowledge-based services.**

RISING FROM THE HIGH SEAS

Around the time I joined EIL, Oil and Natural Gas Corporation, a government of India owned oil company, was exploring in the Arabian Sea, west of *Bombay (now called Mumbai)*. Four years later in 1974, the oil company made history when oil and natural gas gushed out at a high pressure from one of oil wells drilled.

It was a major oil find, in the Arabian Sea, 200 KM west of the city of *Mumbai*. Gradually the oil-field, *then named Bombay High (now called Mumbai High), turned* out to be the biggest oil and gas field ever for India. For at least a decade since then, it changed India's energy scenario satisfying a large part of India's energy and petrochemical demand.

An expansive pipeline network was built later starting from the ocean to mainland India. It carried millions of tons of oil and natural gas resources. A chain of refineries, petrochemical industries and power plants were built to utilize the resources.

But little did I realize that I would be sucked into the Bombay High development project from its very inception. In 1976, I was assigned to Bombay High and its downstream oil and gas processing projects. By the time I left EIL in 1986, a staggering amount of 15-20 billion dollars, perhaps more, had been invested in the chain of major petrochemical and energy infrastructure, spread over India.

My exposure to a number of projects in the chain in some capacity or other became the launching pad for my future.

Here are some anecdotes reflecting the spirit of those days.

*****

AN AMERICAN EXPERIENCE

In the Bombay High development project, the starting point was design, engineering and installation of platforms, supported by steel structures piled beneath the sea. The platforms were to accommodate the equipment and facilities of oil and gas production. There were also pipelines to be laid below the sea to interconnect the platforms and bring oil and natural gas to shore. This part was called *offshore project*.

EIL had no experience of executing offshore projects. With a strong desire to expand into offshore engineering business, the management had built a formidable team of professionals. The team was headed by Dr. Anil Malhotra, a brilliant professional and a leader.

But pre-qualification to offer services required a track record for similar projects as a company. The management signed an agreement of technical collaboration with Crest Engineering of USA, an excellent company with vast experience in such projects. With that, we qualified and got the order.

It was a case of technology absorption. In preparation for it, we did a lot of homework before the start of the project. We made a dummy concept and design for the offshore facilities. We even did some experimental field studies in similar facilities.

After we got the green signal to start the project work, our team from EIL including myself, landed in the office of our collaborator Crest Engineering, at Tulsa (USA).

Initially there seemed to be some barrier and hesitancy of Crest to accept our team as part of theirs. They would let us only review the concepts and design documents they were creating.

In a few weeks' time, the Crest Engineering team presented the oilfield development concept. The concept showed location and layout of the numerous platforms amidst sea, for producing and processing oil and gas, with interconnecting under-the-sea pipelines.

But their concept turned out to be quite different from what we had developed as a *dummy design*!

Soon we understood the reason. Flow of a mixture of crude oil and gas through pipelines is a very complex phenomenon, not following normal rules of fluid flowing in a pipeline. There are multiple choices of design and calculation methodology.

The field work that we had done, helped us to converge on a specific methodology that matched with the data of an existing facility. We found that the methodology of calculations Crest Engineering had chosen was different from ours!

After their presentation was over, I introduced the methodology adopted by us backed up by field data and logic behind it. Then I handed over the presentation of our concept to a young engineer, Dilip, one of my key team members.

Dilip's presentation was confident and overtly aggressive, stressing bluntly that the methodology used by Crest in developing the concept was not applicable in this case.

We all could see the faces of the team of our collaborator gradually turning distinctly grim.

"Who are these guys from an unknown Indian company challenging us?" must have been the thought in their minds!

One thing I always observed in American professionals is that they respect knowledge and logic.

After hearing us, Crest asked for a few days' time to re-examine the issue. They appointed a renowned professor from

Tulsa University specialized in the relevant area for review of methodology used by both sides.

The verdict of the professor was in our favor! Finally, they accepted our concept!

This is not to undermine the capability of Crest, who were far above us in experience and capability of design and implementation of offshore projects. The difference was that their engineer chose a design methodology from the options popping up on the computer, based on their experience in similar projects.

But we, being novices, did a lot of fundamental and experimental studies before choosing the design methodology.

This is one handicap I often find with young engineers of today. They tend to trust the computer blindly without getting into fundamentals!

After this event, we and our American counterparts integrated very well as a team with mutual respect established.

Confident people, they were free and open in transferring knowledge wherever we lacked. It was an ideal Indo-American collaboration which could have seen tremendous long-term benefits to both sides, had the visionaries from both sides continued.

But then.... changes in management occur and visions get lost! Dr. Malhotra, who spearheaded EIL's breakthrough into offshore arena, eventually left the company.

*****

A part of offshore production system (Courtesy: ONGC]

------------------ A Visionary Leader Departs ---------------

Sometime around 1976, our popular chairman Pathak resigned and left for the USA. Why did he leave? The reason was shrouded in doubts as two things happened simultaneously.

Accustomed to take bold actions, Pathak had signed an understanding for joint venture with an oil rich Middle East country. It was based on an initiative taken by the Ministry of External Affairs. It was said that the Ministry of Petroleum under which Engineers India Limited (EIL) operated, did not approve of the decision. Rumors were afloat that Pathak had submitted his resignation as a result of this confrontation.

Another rumor that started floating was that he was suffering from some type of eye problem which needed treatment in the USA. Because of this he was moving to the US to live there.

We had no way to know the real reason. There was a lot of disappointment and dissatisfaction in EIL at the loss of an outstanding leader, loved and admired by the employees.

OVERCOMING THE NAYSAYERS

The Obstacles

The other part of the project, the land-based facility, is an inspiring story of turning the dream of self-reliance into reality.

The facility on the land was to process millions of tons of crude oil and millions of cubic meters of natural gas, flowing in from pipelines laid below the sea. EIL had ample experience and capability on land-based projects. But EIL did not have proven technology of processing natural gas.

Briefly, it involved liquefying the huge volumes of natural gas at high pressure and extremely low temperatures. Then distill out small but valuable part of the gas like LPG (cooking gas) and ethane, a raw material to produce polythene plastics.

The technology was available with many western companies. But well before the start of the project, we had started developing our own know-how and technology in EIL. Before the project started, we were ready. The only snag was that there was no track record of a plant built with our technology.

As expected, there were many naysayers. Many overseas technology companies approached the government of India.

"We have the technology, take it from us. Why spend time re-discovering zero?" was their logic.

"Handling natural gas is hazardous. Don't let the novices design it. Who knows, it may explode," some companies bluntly told our client, Oil and Natural Gas Corporation (ONGC).

Some overseas technology companies directly approached us.

"We give you the technology and let you sign all the design documents. Your name will be there in every design document," they told us.

As if all we wanted was to see our name in print in the design documents!

Many do not understand that the first step towards developing technological capability is to rediscover the zero. That lets you delve deep into the way technology is developed and compare it with existing technologies. That's how Japan and other Asian countries started.

In this case too, we had initiated a lot of investigative work as well as field work related to processing natural gas at very low sub-zero temperatures. We developed some of our own software using computers of the 1970s, of shapes and sizes not imaginable by today's youngsters using laptops.

Our management had developed confidence in our approach and preparedness and convinced the client to award the job to our company. But it came with one condition.

The condition was that once we completed the design, the documents were to be vetted by a reputed international company with substantial experience in designing of similar plants, to certify the design as a safe and workable design.

Soon, we got green signal to start the project. As desired by the client, we got our complete design package vetted by a well-known company in London.

The review by them was smooth. They approved the design **with no major changes!**

*****

------------------Computers of Those Days------------------

Now let me take you on a time travel on working with the computers of the 1960s and 1970s. IBM was one of the pioneers in computing technology and quite predominant in the market. Computers with the accessories including large processors, multiple cassette tapes and disc drives of huge size needed a large hall to accommodate. And it needed an operator.

A computer of the seventies [Courtesy: IBM]

There used to be another room full of equipment, mostly punching machines for input cards. To feed data to run an existing software or for developing a new software, we first wrote the code in FORTRAN language. Then we keyed in the codes in a card punching machine creating a huge bunch of cards with punched slots to feed in. The operator would feed them in the computer and later give us the output.

How fast were those computers? A smartphone of today has more computing power than NASA's 1960s computers for satellite launching.

The Suspense Over a Plant Start-up

It took nearly twenty-four months after the design was approved, to implement the project with engineering, placement of orders for complex equipment and material, construction at site, ensuring QA/QC etc.

Nothing pleases a team of design engineers more than to see their design shooting off the ground as a huge complex of facilities over several hectares of barren land. And performing as per design!

After completion of the construction, we did a series of checks and re-checks at site to ensure everything was in order and take corrective action as needed. Then came the D-Day, start-up of the facility!

It was our first design of a gas processing complex based on our own technology. Would it start smoothly? Would it meet the guarantees on capacity and product quality?

Suspense! Suspense!

Start-up of a process plant, handling hazardous natural gas is in itself a complex and immaculately planned procedure. There are a series of checklists with many action points which are to be ticked off. It is somewhat like the countdown for the launching of a satellite which many may have seen in TV.

It took quite a few days and nights to get the plant started. It was years of hard work nearing fruition. We were on the verge of realizing our dreams! The excitement in our team was quite palpable. We were working in shifts.

My most difficult task was to send back the younger lot after they completed their shift duty. They did not want to miss a single minute of the thrilling process. They would rather continue to stay in the plant site, without sleep, though off-duty!

Part of the Gas Processing Plant [Courtesy: ONGC]

At last, the plant started producing LPG at full design capacity. Samples of LPG were being collected in high pressure steel samplers at fixed intervals for laboratory analysis. That was to check whether it was meeting guaranteed specification.

Someone collected a small sample of LPG in a glass container. It was thrilling to see crystal clear LPG liquid bubbling in the glass container. It is something you never see when liquid LPG in steel cylinders under pressure is delivered to your home as cooking gas.

Sweet smell of success at last! That was when our plant met all guaranteed parameters for specified period of continuous run!

The Sparks That Ignite the Mind

Later we delved deeper into gas processing technology, chilling the gas down to extremely low temperature levels (-100° C). That was required to condense and recover ethane, a valuable raw material to make Polythene plastics. We built numerous gas processing plants based on our own technology.

It is the spark of self-reliance, created by Pathak, our first CEO, that created the fire in the belly. But unfortunately, with passage of time, the fire in the belly often extinguishes.

Perhaps the secret of the most successful companies is to keep the sparks on, like an internal combustion engine of automobiles.

But unlike the engine, it is not automatic sparking with the timer and the circuit! A lot depends on the people who create the sparks – the leaders, who motivate and overcome all obstacles to growth and keep the engine moving!

*****

EXPANDING HORIZONS

With the successful completion of the first phase of Bombay High and interlinked projects, massive expansion took place in the next phases, both offshore and onshore. My continuation with the complete network of projects from the very conceptual stage helped me to expand my horizons.

I recall an incident in the LPG plant described earlier. After the plant was operational, one day I was looking around the plant spread over several hectares. Suddenly I heard my name being announced in the field annunciation system.

"Dr. Dutta, wherever you are, please come to the Control Room immediately," was the announcement I heard from the speakers around.

I rushed to the control room. The top management of our client, ONGC, including Chairman and Managing Director, and our Director (Technical) were in a meeting room adjacent to the control room.

"Welcome Dr. Dutta, we have a crisis," said the Chairman. Then he started describing the problem.

"In the offshore Bombay High platform, the natural gas compressors have to be shut down for a few days, for some emergency maintenance. The supply of gas to the pipeline will stop and pressure of gas reaching our plant will start dropping."

"What will be the impact of the falling gas pressure on LPG production? How long can we operate the plant and supply the gas to the downstream consumers?" he enquired.

The entire visual of the 200 kilometers long sub-sea gas pipeline, over 2 feet in diameter, immediately came to my mind. We old timers, who had grown without calculators in our childhood, are good at mental calculations.

"The volume of pipeline from Bombay High to the LPG plant is a huge reservoir of gas by itself and will act as a buffer," I thought over and replied confidently.

"Fall in pressure will be slow. My rough estimate is that you shall be able to operate the plant efficiently for at least two days without a major fall in LPG production. Downstream consumers of the gas also will not face problem for two days. Please send me the data log of your plant every eight hours and I shall give you a more precise answer by tomorrow."

Quite relieved with my answer, the Chairman looked at his operating staff.

"Keep Dr. Dutta and his team updated on any developments," he ordered authoritatively. "Don't take any decision on any change in plant operating plans without consulting Dr. Dutta."

Such a remark from Chairman of a company may sound sweet to the ears. But I knew it was a compliment to the EIL team. I became a point of recognition of EIL capability.

EIL produced many a professional, whose views were heard with respect by the clients. Frankly, I was happy to have attained the same stature.

*****

THE END OF A PLEASANT JOURNEY

A Taste for Something Different

It was Circa 1986. It was the seventeenth year of my career in EIL. Several mega-projects worth billions of dollars based on our own design and engineering, cropped up from grass roots in front of our eyes. An immensely satisfying journey, it also gave a sense of contributing to India's growth.

All that helped me to gain recognition in the industry. By that time, a number of private companies had cropped up in the oil and natural gas industry. Some started offering me top management positions. But EIL was an organization that grew on us, as we grew with it. It was difficult to think of leaving. And there was a potential for my moving up the management ladder.

The only issue, an important one, was the constraints on power and authority in top management positions in EIL, due to ownership and control by the government. Even our first Chairman, a very dynamic person, had to leave!

During my annual performance review, I discussed the issue frankly with my superior Krishnamurthy.

"One needs to be politically savvy to manage the politicians and government bureaucrats who control the company," he said. It was something I wouldn't enjoy, I felt.

"If you dream of doing something different with freedom, then go for a change," he advised.

I always had an urge to experiment with new and different things. Looking back, that session of annual review triggered an inexplicable urge to take a plunge to do something different.

Exactly at the same time something happened by strange coincidence. *Destiny gave me an interesting choice.*

Sharma, a friend of mine, was at the time the Chief Executive of CE Natco International, Singapore, a company owned by Combustion Engineering Inc. (CE) of USA. Quite unlike EIL, Natco was not a service provider. It had some special technology for certain sub-systems of oil and natural gas processing. Based on the technology, Natco manufactured and delivered skid mounted equipment package.

Sharma used to occasionally drop in at my home during his business trips to India for a friendly tete-a-tete. During one such visit, he told me that Natco wanted to set up an India office. He was looking for someone to take charge and develop its presence in India.

Then he took me by surprise.

"Utpal, what about you taking charge? You think it over and we shall discuss during my next visit," he said.

Sharma told me that my mandate would be to establish Natco as a company in India and secure a substantial market share.

The very thought of doing something different from what I was doing made the idea exciting to me. And having my trusted friend Sharma as my link to Natco was a comforting thought.

I decided to take the plunge. I submitted my resignation by the end of 1986.

The Pains of Parting

Parting with EIL after nearly two decades was very painful!

To most of us, EIL was not just a work place. The experience we got was unique. It not only gave us depth in the specific discipline of engineering. It added further dimensions to it through continuous interaction with engineers of multiple disciplines, team work and management interactions.

It was an Alma Mater to us!

The uniqueness of this experience is borne out by the fact that several American consultancy companies used to camp in New Delhi every year, for walk-in interviews to grab EIL Engineers.

"You never really leave the place you love. You take part of it with you and leave part of you there," I read somewhere.

I know a part of EIL is still with me. But I realized that a part of me was still there, when I visited EIL two decades later in 2007 with an ex-EIL colleague. It was to conduct a training program.

I was really overwhelmed by the tumultuous welcome with love and respect showered on us. It was somewhat like the return of family members who had left home long back! It really felt like homecoming. And just imagine, after two decades of gap, I hardly knew the faces around me, barring a few!

I was really lucky to have worked in a company I found so hard to say goodbye to! It gave me the confidence to move on to new paths of corporate adventures.

CHAPTER - 2

A TRIAL BY FIRE

INITIATION IN SOLITUDE

"Today I close the door to my past, open the door to my future, take a deep breath, and step through a new life."

~ Anonymous

It was sometime in late 1986 that I left EIL and joined CE Natco, a multinational American company. Sharma, my friend and CEO of Natco, Singapore, had assigned me the task of setting up Natco business in India.

India was not a business-friendly country in the 1980's, particularly for foreign companies. Registering Natco as a company immediately was out of question. Forming a joint venture with an Indian company was a possible solution. But it would take time. We had to find some a way for a quick start.

To start with, there was a need for an office for me. Sharma located a one room office for me to start with. Combustion Engineering Inc., had a small office space for its subsidiaries in a five-star hotel-cum-office complex in New Delhi. Natco being one of their companies, they agreed to accommodate me in an unoccupied room under some financial arrangement.

"Utpal, this is your office. I just don't know what you have to do. You have to find out what you want to do," was the parting remark of Sharma!

The first day in that office sitting all alone in a large room with five-star furnishing was an unforgettable experience. Only a few days back I was in the hustle and bustle of EIL office full of thousands of engineers and other staff. Now suddenly I was in total solitude!

The future looked like a trial by fire for me, the thrill of which I found to be very motivating!

Sitting there all alone, the cobwebs of my thoughts on how to develop Natco in India started getting cleared. By the end of the day, I had a reasonably clear plan for the path ahead.

It was a good day's job done sitting quietly in solitude, *doing nothing!*

My initial focus was on the Western region of India, including Bombay High offshore fields., which was my playing field during the last two decades. There were ample opportunities there for skid mounted equipment based on Natco's technology. The oilfields were owned mostly by Oil & Natural Gas Corporation, popularly known as ONGC.

Keeping the dialogue on with contacts is a very important component to start a business. I called and fixed a few meetings with my contacts in ONGC and some other companies in the city of Vadodara in the state of Gujarat. Vadodara was a hub for oil and gas industry in the western region.

"You are moving from a large company to a small company, almost non-existent here," some of my friends warned me when I left EIL. "It will be difficult for you to get the same kind of access to the top management of your clients as you were getting as a senior executive in EIL," they said.

But I faced no such problem. Rather I received a very uplifting remark from someone in a very senior management position in one of the oil companies. I had fixed a meeting with him in my hotel at Vadodara for a Friday morning breakfast meet.

He called me while I was in Vadodara and told me that due to unforeseen engagements, it would not be possible for him to meet me on either Friday or Saturday.

"What about lunch with me on Sunday, 1 p.m.?" I asked him. He hesitated for a moment and then replied in the affirmative.

When we met for lunch on Sunday, the very first comment he made boosted my mood!

"Dr. Dutta, my wife was surprised that I was going out for a business lunch on a Sunday," he said. "I normally spend every Sunday lunch time with my family. I explained to her that the gentleman who has called me is such a person that I just can't refuse to meet him."

In life, you get both criticisms and compliments. I tend to take both coolly. But frankly, as a lone ranger for Natco, I relished his statement. It reassured me that during my two decades of work, I had earned goodwill from my clients.

After the meetings I got a clear idea of the prospects in that region and firmed up my strategy. Not yet registered as a company, I could not bid for the projects directly. As a short-term strategy, I planned to provide back up of Natco technology to potential Indian bidders. The longer-term strategy was to establish Natco as a joint venture company in India,

I took a deep breath and stepped into a new journey, in full throttle.

*****

The Virtues of Doing Nothing

I have intentionally used a phrase 'doing nothing' at some point in the preceding episode. I recall an incident in one of the busiest periods my career. One day my daughter asked me, "What do you love to do most?"

Prompt came my reply, "I love doing nothing."

After a few weeks she suddenly appeared with a Sunday magazine section of The Times of India, a newspaper. She pointed to an article where the author interviewed several prominent persons on what they love doing most.

To my surprise, many of them answered, "I love doing nothing!"

While doing nothing you are not really doing nothing. You are letting your subconscious work out solutions and ideas. The best period of doing nothing is a good night's sleep, which clears a lot of your cobwebs.

FROM THE OTHER SIDE OF THE TABLE

[Names of some companies and characters in this episode have been changed]

Soon after joining, I made my first attempt at securing a major work order for Natco. My erstwhile employer Engineers India Ltd. (EIL) had floated a request for quotation on behalf of an oil producing company in India. It was for a sizable number of crude oil treatment equipment packages, in line with the kind of technology-based equipment package Natco was known for.

I decided to tie-up with a major equipment fabrication company, let us call Mumbai Fabricators Limited (name changed).

The strategy was that Mumbai Fabricators will pre-qualify as the bidder for the job, with the backup of Natco's technology. Natco's role would be design with guarantees, with supply of some critical hardware components by Natco Singapore.

Verma (name changed) was the Business Development Manager of Mumbai Fabricators at that time. We knew each other quite well. We made an effective combination. We analyzed the enquiry document in detail, worked out the strategy and the pricing.

Our bid was submitted in two parts as required – 'Technical Bid' with all technical details and a sealed 'Commercial Bid' with pricing and commercial terms. The commercial bid was to be opened after the technical bid was vetted and qualified by EIL.

Technical evaluation started with 'technical questionnaire' issued to all bidders by EIL.

For the first time I was on the other side of the table at EIL office!

Being part of the system earlier, I knew the kind of questions that would come. It would be a series of questions deeply probing into the technology aspect of the equipment, which no bidder would be ready to divulge. But not answering them under the cover of trade secret or patent could lead to disqualification.

The art in answering them was to tell the truth but not the whole truth.

There were seven bidders to start with. Each one was bombarded with numerous technical queries. We received a set of 30 technical queries. Majority of them probed deep into the technology and methodology of design.

I was sure Natco would never answer most of them, even at the risk of losing the opportunity. I sent the questions to Natco office in Singapore and as expected most of the queries remained unanswered.

I decided that the best way to answer all the queries was from theoretical and fundamental engineering principles and qualify the answers with the rider - "The final design is calibrated based on Natco's experience and practices using empirical factors, which are proprietary information."

I did accordingly and it seemed to be working. There were several volleys of counter questions and answers, before EIL took the final decision to technically qualify or reject the bidders.

The results were announced – out of seven bidders four were rejected and three qualified technically. We were one of the three!

Now soon the priced bids would be opened. Verma and I met to discuss the next step.

"Dr. Dutta, you have played your part well and brought the ball near the goal post," he told me. "I have to dribble through the two competitors and shoot the goal now."

"But how?" I asked.

"One of our two competitors is a very big company with a wide range of products. They have been mostly higher than us in the biddings in the past. Moreover, my feedback is that their fabrication yard is fully booked and overloaded. I don't think they will pose a problem to us," he explained.

"What about the second competitor whom I know to be a small company?" I asked.

"I have already set up my strategy for them." He said confidently.

"As you know, there is always a mandatory meeting in EIL between Project, Engineering and Procurement Departments before opening a sealed priced bid. I shall make sure someone in the meeting raises a strong doubt about capability of the small fabrication facility of our competitor," he said confidently.

"A decision will be taken in the meeting to send an inspector to visit and evaluate the fabrication shop for its capability," he continued. "It is a grey area, a borderline situation. The person visiting the shop has to make up his mind to say *yes or no*."

There was a pregnant pause!

Then he gave a firm and climactic statement, poker-faced.

"I shall help the person make up his mind."

Subsequent events happened exactly the same way. The smaller company was disqualified. Only two were left in the run. The prices were opened. As expected, we were lower in price and won the contract.

The joys of victory at the very first attempt was marred a bit as my image of EIL took a beating. Working in EIL with a team committed to the ideals of achieving self-reliance on technology, a very idealistic image of EIL had been embedded in my mind.

For the first time I saw EIL from the other side of the table.

I realized that even in company like EIL, there were some dark corners where people can be 'helped to make up their mind' by outsiders. Though I must state here that EIL inspection and certification group is regarded very trustworthy and ethical by Indian and global companies.

I realized that dark corners can be there in any company. The ground realities of the business world started to dawn on me with this incident.

*****

IN FULL SWING

A Quick Breakthrough

After the success of securing the first major order, the word spread that CE Natco of USA is here in India going in full gallop. Within a short time, we landed into four major projects.

Unexpected help from my network of contacts, reputation of Natco as a technology-based company and a bit of luck, all worked together in our favor.

I got a lead from someone that an oil company was negotiating a contract with Project Construction Limited (name changed), an engineering and construction company. The contract was to build four major crude oil processing plants on turnkey basis, covering design, engineering, supply of equipment, installation of the entire plant and commissioning.

I promptly met someone I knew well in the top management of the oil company. I expressed interest for some role for Natco in these projects. He knew about Natco capabilities quite well.

"Well, you fit in very well there," he said. "Some of the equipment in crude oil processing need proprietary technology where Natco can fill the gap. In fact, one of the conditions in our contract is for Project Construction Ltd. (PCL) to take technology backup for such equipment."

"Natco has all the relevant technologies," I assured him.

He picked up the phone and called someone in PCL. He spoke to him to consider Natco as a possible contender for technology backup.

The very next day I got a call from PCL.

"Dr. Dutta, our General Manager Mr. Benjamin (name changed) is in New Delhi. He would like to meet you at his hotel over breakfast tomorrow morning," the caller informed.

Our meeting went off well. We knew each other though we had not worked together in any project. He knew about Natco too. He was one of those rare bold executives, capable of taking fast decisions to act upon. Things started moving at jet speed!

"There is no time to waste," Bejamin said. "Rumors have spread that the oil company is going to award us these projects on negotiated basis. Our competitors will soon start lobbying to stall the move. Let us sign an agreement and jointly meet the management of the oil company tomorrow," he stated.

We discussed the terms of the agreement and reached a consensus. Before the end of the day, a collaboration agreement was signed by both of us. It was perhaps the speediest conclusion of a commercial agreement!

We met the Director (Projects) of the oil company the very next day. He expressed satisfaction over our collaboration.

Benjamin made sure that the contract with the oil company was finalized quickly. All done before our competitors could bat an eyelid! Soon the oil company awarded the contract for four major projects to PCL on turnkey basis.

Natco became the associate of PCL to provide technology backup and supply of critical equipment for all four projects! It was a major breakthrough for Natco in the Indian market

I came to know later that Benjamin was warned by the Board of Directors of PCL, for having signed an agreement with Natco without their approval. I am sure he knew the risk of bypassing procedures of a large company. But fortunately, he took the risk and moved fast to close the deal with the oil coompany!

Giving a Shape to Natco

With sizable orders already in bag, my next step was to quickly get a platform for Natco India to execute the job.

Meanwhile, the CEO of Taylor Instruments India Ltd., an Indian joint venture company of Combustion Engineering Inc, was keeping his eyes open for new business opportunities. He used to meet me often in my office.

The moment he heard of the opportunity created by Natco, he proposed a mutually beneficial solution.

"See, Natco and Taylor Instruments India are both owned by Combustion Engineering Inc. We are sister companies," he said. "Taylor Instruments India is already registered as an Indian company and has approval from government for this kind of equipment systems business," he confirmed.

"Why not set up Natco business as a part of Taylor Instruments? It will not require any approval from the government. We can create a Natco Division as a profit center of Taylor Instrument," he proposed.

I had some reservations. The Indian partner of the Taylor Instruments joint venture was a large family-owned business house, which owned many companies. Natco business would be just a small part of it.

But it was the only solution for Natco to start quickly in India. The management of Natco Singapore approved the idea. A Natco Division office was set up by Taylor immediately. I took charge of the Natco Division. PCL subcontracted the Natco's scope for all the four projects to Taylor Instruments.

Natco was in full swing within a short time from its inception!

------------------How to Get Paid by Clients------------------

One of the difficult aspects of business in India has always been recovery of the payments due from some of the clients. When the client company withholds payments to the prime contractor, it creates a chain effect of delayed payments to the subcontractors of goods and services. Such situations were sometimes intentionally created due to vested interests.

In the afore-mentioned projects, PCL was the prime contractor and we Taylor Instruments India Ltd.-Natco Division, were subcontractor for goods and services.

After substantial progress in the job, we raised our first invoice to PCL. Months passed without any payment. The finance department of Taylor Instruments kept reminding them. PCL maintained the stand that the oil company, their client, had not paid them on their invoices yet and the moment they get paid, they would clear our invoice.

Quite a few months went by like that. One day I got a frantic call from my friend Bejamin of PCL.

"Dr. Dutta, please do me a favor. Your Taylor Instruments management has sent a gentleman who is sitting in our reception for the last three days continuously. He says he won't move till he gets the payments due. Please, please ask your management to take him off. I assure that even if we don't get the payment from our client, I shall pay you within a week."

I conveyed the message to the Head of Finance in Taylor. His man was called back. Within a week we got the payments.

AN EXEMPLARY STORY OF NEGOTIATION

We had submitted our quote for an interesting project for a privately owned company. After the client scrutinized the bid, two companies were shortlisted by them for final negotiation. One of them was our company Taylor-Natco.

One of my weakest points has been dislike for commercial negotiation. In developing business for my company, I continued to take the initiatives to the point of being called for final negotiation. But going for negotiation was an absolute "no, no" for me. So, I decided to send one of my executives, who in my esteem appeared to be a good negotiator.

We analyzed our pricing estimate thoroughly and concluded that it was a very competitive price. If at all we had to yield under pressure, the maximum discount could be 7.5%.

The client's office was in another city, Vadodara. On a prescheduled date, my executive left for Vadodara, where we were called for negotiation. Our competitor was also called for the negotiation on the same day. The negotiations went on till late night. I waited anxiously. After 10.00 PM, I got a call from our man that we have bagged the order.

The next day, he came to the office and gave an interesting blow by blow account of how the negotiations went. Let me put the story as told by him, speaking in the first person.

"I reached our client's office at the scheduled time of 11.00 AM. I was asked to sit and wait in one corner of a large waiting hall. I found our competitors, two of their men, sitting in another corner of the hall, discussing something in hushed voices.

"They kept us waiting for quite some time. You see your competitors in the other corner and keep waiting. Perhaps that was one of the ways to wear us out before the negotiations start!

"After an hour or so they called our competitors first. Another phase of waiting! After they came out, I was called in.

"The discussion hovered around for some time on technical part of the proposal. It was short and they seemed to be very satisfied with the technical part of the proposal. Then the real thing started– the commercial part.

"They started with the statement that our price was high. They discussed some items of cost which we had put under the head 'Client's Responsibility' for logical reasons. They asked me to include those in our scope. I asked for some time to look into it.

"They agreed and announced a break for lunch stating that the meeting would continue from 4.00 PM. As I came out from the room, I had a hunch that they were reasonably satisfied with the pricing of our proposal.

"At 4.00 PM we were back in the waiting hall. After another round of discussion with our competitor, they called me in. I responded to the earlier queries on adjustment of some commercial scope. Then they asked me to give our final price with a discount. They stated firmly that they would decide today itself based on the final prices of the two competitors.

"They gave both the parties one-hour time to think, speak to our management if necessary and give the final price in writing.

"I came out and saw some discussions taking place in hushed voice between the two executives of our competitor in the other corner. It was not audible at all from the distance. I decided to use the toilet which was located midway.

"The discussion stopped as they saw me approaching the toilet!

"I went in and took quite some time inside the toilet, hoping discussions between them would resume. Later as I was coming out, I heard a whisper, 'the lowest price we can give is ………'

"Whatever I heard was higher than what we had quoted! But that was a feel, I really did not hear it so clearly.

"I sat down and tried to recall every word during the discussion I had during the day. My hunch grew stronger that both technically and commercially our bid was attractive to them. The whisper that I overheard strengthened my hunch. Should I give a discount? My hunch said no.

"But then a fear came over me – management had given me freedom of up to 7.5% discount. If I do not use it and lose the job, how do I explain it? I made up my mind not to yield except for a token discount of 2.5% *'to honor of the request made by the client.'*

"Around 6 PM our competitors were called and they gave their final prices in writing. Then I was called and I wrote exactly what my hunch told me. In the next one hour the client team called me inside.

"They shook hands and handed over a letter of intent on award of the contract!"

*****

---------------------The Art of Negotiation--------------------

Three important attributes of a good negotiator are listening, patience to hold your ground and emotional intelligence (you can call it hunch). Our man displayed all the three attributes in this negotiation.

I avoid getting into negotiations because patience to hold your ground during commercial negotiation has never been a strong point with me. Perhaps it is due to one of my childhood experiences.

In India, negotiation with street vendors or even in shops is quite common. In childhood whenever we went shopping with my parents, I used to watch them bargain over the price, often beating down the seller to a much lower price. I used to get bored, impatient and tired. Often my sympathies used to go to the seller.

A TURN OF EVENTS

At this point, I cannot help quoting from a cartoon I still remember.

A loyal employee resigns. The boss, quite surprised, calls him to his office and asks, "Why?" Prompt comes the reply from the employee who had made up his mind, *"I would like to stay, Sir. But time is running out if I want to start a Rock Group."*

It was Circa 1990. I had joined Natco in 1986 in the solitude of an empty room with no employee. And now I was under the umbrella of a giant family business house, running Natco Division as a profit center. Job orders were healthy. I had built up a team of young engineers.

There was no need for me to think of a change in the immediate future, though I had no intent to stay on for too long.

Yes, there were some lacunae. In one of the preceding sections, I mentioned that Taylor India was part of a giant Indian family run business house – something I had not bargained for. I always had a penchant for a free hand, which was not tenable as a part of a large company.

"You can't always wait for the perfect time. Sometimes, you have to dare to do it because life is too short to wonder what could have been," I had read somewhere.

At this stage, certain incidents and coincidences happened in a way as if destiny was pushing me towards a *choice* I wanted to take! You can see all that happen as you flip to the next chapter.

"You don't build business, you build people. Then people build the business."

– Zig Ziglar, An American Author

CHAPTER - 3

THE THRILLS OF A START-UP

THE GENESIS

A Man for All Seasons

Binoy Jacob had met me a few times during my tenure at Engineers India Ltd. (EIL) during the 1980's. His profile is interesting. Trained in hospitality management after his degree in Economics from a prominent institute, he climbed up the corporate ladder pretty fast as General Manager in a five-star hotel in New Delhi.

In the pinnacle of his career with innumerable luxuries, he decided to leave the cushy job! He started representing a few major American technology companies in the energy and petrochemical sector, at a nominal monthly retainer.

It was a quite unusual movement – from hotel industry to **technology business!**

Even when I moved to Natco, he used to keep in touch. I knew very little about him except that he had become quite successful in his marketing ventures.

Sometime in 1989, he took me by surprise with a proposal.

"Utpal, you had been executing major projects in your previous company EIL. Would you be interested in creating a company like that from scratch?" It was a probing question!

"I have a plan to start a new company providing engineering consultancy services in the pattern of EIL or Lummus of USA," he continued. "I shall be presenting my ideas at Oberoi Intercontinental. I have invited senior management people from different industries. Would you like to attend the meeting?"

The idea sounded interesting. I decided to attend the meeting without any intent of leaving Natco at that time.

It was a clear and crisp presentation of his dream project. He presented the market scenario with specific focus on South East Asia, which was booming at that time. He highlighted the idea that it was an opportune moment to start an engineering services company in oil, gas and power sector. He exuded confidence and displayed knowledge of the nuances of the relevant industries.

We met quite a few times after that at his favorite Oberoi Intercontinental Hotel. With close interactions during the meeting, I felt that he was a person I could trust. He seemed keen that I join him to start and develop his dream project.

The idea of a start up from scratch thrilled me. But I was reasonably happy with what I was doing for Natco.

And there was one insurmountable barrier. My friend Sharma, of Natco Singapore, had given me the responsibility of developing Natco in India. The sapling that we planted together as Natco India was about to enter its adulthood. To give it up midway was morally not possible for me.

In the beginning of the book, I talked about destiny, choice and creating your own destiny by your choice. Unusual **coincidences happen sometimes in life!**

A few weeks after meeting with Jacob, Sharma called me.

"Utpal, there is a news which may surprise you," he said. "I have resigned from Natco Singapore and shall be joining another company soon."

That single statement cleared my path. I called Jacob the next day and told him that I was willing to join. We met in his home the next day to complete our *understanding*. The die was cast. In January 1990 we registered a company based on our vision. We named it *Triune Projects Private Limited,* known as **Triune**.

He offered me a nominal but worthwhile equity in Triune as an incentive. While running Natco business, I had realized that my clients had goodwill towards me. I felt that having equity in the company, however small it might be, may translate some of that goodwill to the company too.

This was the beginning of a thrilling story. There was no written understanding between us. We both were driven by mutual trust and a common vision to create an outstanding engineering consultancy company in the oil and gas sector. The relationship remains intact even now, overcoming the vagaries of time.

A very interesting and smart person, he understood people. He was equally at ease with a child or someone far senior to him or a pretty young girl or an elderly lady, a poor unskilled worker or a rich business tycoon. How do you describe such a person? The sub-title at the beginning says it all.

Charting the Path Forward

"The elevator to success is out of order. You have to use the stairs... one step at a time."

~ Joe Girard

My assignment in Triune was an altogether different ball game from my previous assignment of establishing Natco in India!

Natco was an internationally known company in the oil and gas business with a formidable track record and proprietary technology. But Triune was a case of start-up from scratch!

A few of my ex-colleagues and friends thought joining an unknown entity was an error of judgment on my part, which might ruin my career. Some wryly commented that who would give a job to a single man company?

But often a single man outfit gets important consultancy jobs if the person is credible. I was confident that I would be able to get some jobs on my own.

To make Triune look better than a single man company, I tied up with a few of my ex-colleagues. They were working as freelancers, and were well-known faces in the industry. With their consent, I included their profile in our company brochure.

Jacob had meanwhile built his corporate office in a business-cum shopping complex in Delhi for his marketing and other business outfits. It was a beautiful office with space to accommodate 40 to 50 seats, mostly lying empty.

He accommodated me in the office with an evocative remark, "Utpal, fill up all the empty spaces."

Over a period, a three-prong strategy evolved in my mind.

First – Start with consultancy orders of small sizes, but significant content to establish credibility, get cash-flow and expand manpower.

Second – Target total engineering and project management services from concept to commissioning of small to medium size projects. Gradually step up the size of jobs.

Third – Target overseas jobs which fetch far better returns.

But hold on! This three-prong strategy did not evolve overnight like a magic. It evolved over the initial period of client interaction and business development efforts.

It is important not to be rigid about such plans in the growth stage. Grab the opportunities as they come!

"Use the stairs, one step at a time" - yes. But unlike the stairs, I thought, each step should be higher than the previous one!

*****

---Airlines and Engineering Consultancy Company---

Both are essentially people-oriented service industries. Airlines have individual passengers and corporates as their clients. Engineering consultancy companies have operating companies as clients. But there is a major difference.

When you select, book and board an airline you don't know who are the pilots and stewards or who is the General Manager of the airline. It is a kind of service where familiarity with a 'face' is not important.

But in engineering service industry, 'face' matters a lot in building a 'brand'. A project execution takes years of interaction between the client and the consultant. The client's familiarity and confidence on the key people they would be dealing with, matter a lot. They want to know who would be the project manager or construction manager and sometimes may even demand that a specific person in the company lead the charge.

This perspective was told to me years later by an outstanding management person, P. K. Rudra. In retrospect, while developing Triune, we followed the same principle. We could induct right 'faces' in the right time which was one of the key factors that lead to a successful start-up of Triune.

A TODDLER'S FIRST STEPS (1990-1993)

The Three 'C's Towards Success

There is a saying that for business development you need three 'C's - *contact, contact and contact*. For our kind of knowledge-based service industry, I would modify it to say that the three 'C's you need are *Contact, Credibility (meaning credible 'Faces') and Confidence.*

Getting the first few orders quickly was very important. And difficult too.

Without using any further management jargon, let me exemplify with a few interesting stories of winning consultancy orders of high quality from major companies in the beginning. That helped the new born baby grow into a Toddler.

To Search a Needle in a Haystack

In one of my first business development forays, I started meeting a senior executive of a major petroleum refining company. We knew each other well. The refining company had several petroleum refineries in India. They often required services like feasibility studies and debottlenecking studies for their refineries, which suited us.

I briefed him frankly about our strength, capabilities and plans. He asked me some questions and then suggested an exciting opening for us.

"I have one enquiry which I can give you," he said. "I know you can do it. But our management has more or less made up their mind to award it to Engineers India Ltd (EIL)."

"We can definitely beat EIL at the pricing and do a quality job," I replied.

"I know you can. But that's not the point," he explained. "The job requires highly specialized knowledge. It is for a feasibility study, preliminary design and project report for production of micro-crystalline wax in one of our refineries."

Refineries rarely produce micro-crystalline wax. Very few people are knowledgeable about it. But the crude oil the refinery was processing is an excellent source for it. Only EIL had done a similar project for them earlier.

"But there must be others in India knowledgeable about it. We have enough contacts to search and outsource expertise from elsewhere." I replied.

"Yes, that's what I was coming to," he said. "Frankly, the key people who worked for EIL in this project have all left. The key process technology man there was a guy named Gaurav *(name changed)*. If you can locate him and get him in your team, I can justify to the management on giving the job to you."

"We were planning to award the job to EIL next week," he continued, while pulling out a paper.

"Here is your enquiry. You have only a few days to locate Gaurav, get his written consent to work with you on this project and submit your proposal with a competitive price."

I knew Gaurav who had joined as a graduate trainee in EIL during my tenure there. Where to locate him? I immediately rushed straight to EIL office and met some of his friends. They helped me with his home address.

His home was in the city of Vadodara, one and a half hours' flight from Delhi. I called a contact of mine at Vadodara. I gave him the address and asked him to search him out quickly.

Remember, it was the year 1991. Internet was just coming up and was not yet so widespread. Cellphones had just started in the USA and not known yet in India. Communication was not easy. Particularly so in India of those days.

Next morning, I got a call from my Vadodara contact which was not so encouraging. Gaurav's house was locked. Neighbors informed that he was doing social work, living in his ancestral village. All that I got was the name of the village, one of a million or so remote and unknown villages in India.

With only a few more days in hand, at first it sounded like searching for a needle in a haystack.

But with a little thinking I got my search-lines right!

The best way to communicate fast in India those days was *'telegram'*, a telegraphic message from post and telegraph office. It was the only form of communication that managed to reach the remotest parts of India and was dependable.

I rushed to a nearby post and telegraph office and drafted a telegram to Gaurav with the details. As for his address, I had nothing except his name and the village name. I surmised that in a small village he would be a person prominent enough.

The officer at the telegraph office informed me that there was no telegraph office in the village. He asked me to give the location of a telegraph office nearest to his village.

I had no idea! I requested him to help. He pulled out a thick printed directory, flipped through it and located the nearest telegraph office. I made payments and came back to my office hoping for the best. It was around 2.00 PM by then.

Early next morning, the doorbell of my home rang. I opened the door and found a man in uniform had come to deliver a telegram in my name. The message was from Gaurav!

It said, "Thanks for your message. Agree to work for you. Shall come to Delhi and meet you by tomorrow evening." The Indian Telegraph Services did not fail!

The very next day, Gaurav and I met my contact at Indian Oil.

You can conclude the rest of the story!

The Case of the Three Quotations

Satyajit Ray, a world-famous film director, had during his life time created epic films covering various aspects of life in India with universal appeal.

At the start of this story, I can't help recalling a scene from his famous award-winning movie *'Jana Aranya'* (titled *'The Middleman'* in English - though not a literal translation of the title).

An educated unemployed youngster, looking for a job, accidentally comes across a businessman. The businessman feels pity on him and advises him to start his own business.

"But how?" he asks.

"Here is my business card. Come and see me in my office tomorrow," he tells the young man.

The youngster visits his office as scheduled and enters his glass walled cabin. In front of his cabin was a huge hall, full of rows of tables and chairs laid all along, mostly occupied by one or two persons.

"You have a really big office, sir!" The youngster exclaimed.

"No," the businessman replied, "I have leased out almost all the office area to these people. Each person sitting in front of a table is running businesses. I provide administrative and other support, help them grow business and charge for it. You too will do business from here, occupying one of the empty tables."

"But how?" the youngster asked, quite baffled!

"I shall tell you." The businessman replied.

He called his assistant and told him, "Register three companies for him. And print business cards for all the three."

"Three companies?" the youngster asked, totally baffled again!

"Yes," the businessman replied. "Yes, that is the minimum number you require to start your business. You see the gentleman sitting there? He has seven companies!"

"You will start with the business of buying stationary from wholesale market and supply at a higher price to different business houses. You will be *the middleman*. I shall give you a few of my contacts in the industry. But they will ask you to help them get three quotations to justify ordering on you. That's why you need three companies," he explained.

This preamble was required because here is a parallel story on what I had to do to get a legitimate order from a client, though not as a 'Middleman'.

During my heydays in EIL, I was the team leader for design and execution of a major natural gas processing plant near Mumbai. I had close interaction with many of the engineers of the owner's operating team.

One day in my Triune office I got a call from the gas processing plant. The caller introduced himself as Nathan asked, "Do you remember me?"

"Yes, of course," I said. I recalled that he was one of the bright young fellows in the Plant owner's team.

"I am now heading the Plant you designed. I want to increase the capacity of the Plant at a minimum cost with a de-bottlenecking and troubleshooting study on the Plant," he said.

"Can you take it up?" he asked.

"Of course," I replied. "I shall send one of my engineers to look into the scope of work and then submit our quotation,"

"Okay," he said. "I can consider placing the job order to your company under the condition that you will personally guide the engineer doing the work."

I assured him it would be like that.

Our engineer visited the plant site and worked out a scope of work. We conveyed the budgetary price for doing the job along with the scope of work.

He called me a few days later.

"Dr. Dutta, your price is reasonable," he said. "I am ready to pay the price. But you have to get me quotations from at least two other well-recognized consultancy companies, with prices higher than yours. I cannot order at this level of price without three quotations. And you have to keep some margin in your price so that I can negotiate."

Immediately I recalled the episode from the Ray's film and was really laughing inside. I never could imagine someday I might have to face a situation to produce three quotations!

Anyway, I had enough friends in the industry running consultancy businesses. I chose a few trustworthy ones out of them, took them in confidence. I sent the name, address and credentials of two companies to our prospective client.

It made a total of three companies to bid including ours.

We all quoted. Ours was the lowest! We got the order!

These are only a few examples of the heroics we had to do to start a company with no track record and no manpower base. In both cases, *'contact'* as well as *'face'* were important.

Multiple job orders, from different industry sectors and of different scope, were the first small steps towards our vision to create an engineering consultancy company, providing comprehensive services, from concept to commissioning.

*****

The Young Guns

At the very start, I was fortunate that some young engineers who knew me, decided to risk their career by leaving reputed companies to join Triune. Instead of confusing the readers with too many names, let me call them The Young Guns.

The Young Guns made enormous contribution within their limited experience. Their contribution was not only in job execution but also in creating new opportunities. After a year or two of getting the intense start-up exposure, some of them left for greener pastures! I call it, 'the collateral damage'!

I am happy to see years later, some of them either turning up as successful entrepreneurs or occupying top management positions in major companies.

One of the young guns is now CEO of Triune!

CASTING THE FOUNDATION

The job orders started flowing in, gradually going up in size, range of services and value of the fees. We generated cash inflow and created a good reference of around twenty job orders from major companies in the very first year of our inception.

Simultaneously, the process of adding manpower and building the organization was on. Often one lands in a dilemma of *chicken or egg situation* – jobs first or manpower first?

But we never worried about it. Fortunately, one followed the other in very quick sequence, almost as if in parallel.

I started inducting quite a few of senior professionals with high credibility in the industry from the very first year. It was important to raise the 'face' value of the company (pun intended) at some risk of high operating cost.

Both, Jacob and I, converged in our ideas. A formidable top management team was created within a few years.

The foundation was thus cast for growth and realizing our vision of creating the first privately owned, high-end engineering consultancy company in India in the Oil & Gas sector.

The Team at the Top

Time to introduce the top management team that we could build within the first two or three years.

First to join was Mathur, my ex-colleague from EIL. A top-notch project manager, he had decades of experience of managing major projects for offshore oil and gas industry.

Mathur took charge as our Head of Projects. A systematic man with a penchant for perfection, he aptly compensated for my wayward undisciplined nature.

Then came Amal, another ex-colleague from my erstwhile employer EIL. A committed person with decades of experience in process technology, he had good links with major petroleum refineries. He took charge of our Process Design Department.

An interesting induction was Rai (name changed). Alas, he is no more! Triune and I owe a lot to his efforts.

A senior engineering professional from Power Industry, he was a man of exceptional versatility. In the organization, he could fit into any slot. We put him as Head of Finance and Administration, including HRD. With the appearance of a hard exterior, though sensitive inside, he fitted very well in my scheme of things. I had a persuasive approach to our employees. Rai willingly became the hard face of the company.

Sud, another addition from my ex-company, was an outstanding engineering manager with decades of experience in EIL and other major companies. He joined as Head of Engineering. A calm and gentle person, he had a steel like firmness in approach, hidden behind his gentle appearance. Honest to the core, he was my alter ego.

As the CEO of the company, I had to take decisions sometimes harsh and unfair to our competitors, much to my discomfort. Had I not taken the task of developing Triune from scratch, I would have chosen his way.

Above all of us was Basu. Senior-most amongst us by age, he was a doyen in the oil and gas industry in India. I said *above all of us* because to numerous people in the industry in India, he was respected as *'Dada'*, meaning elder brother. The only problem was that to help his 'younger brothers' in different companies, he occasionally took actions detrimental to our interest!

Last but not the least was Jacob, the confident and erudite entrepreneur, owner of the company. I discussed the induction of all the senior professionals with him. He backed me up on whatever I did, sometimes disagreeing but never obstructing.

It was a formidable management team by any standards. As a layer of icing over the cake, most of us had worked together as a team in our erstwhile company EIL.

Within a few years of inception, Triune had grown from a few to nearly one hundred technical personnel in size, moving towards a turnover of nine-digit figure in Rupees. A good organization structure took shape.

*****

ANECDOTES ON LANDMARK EVENTS

The anecdotes are about two interesting project orders - one of them in the area of petroleum refining and the other in the area of oil and gas processing. These were our first two projects, covering the entire range of services from concept to commissioning. The jobs helped us cast the foundation of creating an engineering consultancy company to reckon with.

Pleasure to Work With

We competed with my erstwhile company Engineers India Limited and got our first order with comprehensive engineering and project execution services. It was a revamp of a plant in a refinery complex, owned by Bharat Petroleum Corporation Limited (BPCL) in Mumbai. Though in terms of value it was not big, its importance to us was immense. It was our first refinery job order based on our *technology and performance guarantee.*

Everything moved smoothly as long as all the basic design and engineering work was being done from within our office in New Delhi. Engineering activity was completed and all equipment were ordered as per our planned schedule.

Then the work moved outside our office. The activities were inspection and quality assurance with equipment suppliers. It was to ensure that the manufacturing process was progressing as per schedule, meeting the quality. The term used for this activity is "Inspection and Expediting." Construction at plant site, another out of the office activity, had also started.

A regular monthly project review meeting took place at the office of the General Manager of our client BPCL. Our Head of Projects, Mathur, used to lead our team in the meetings. He used to regularly brief me about the developments.

Before one such meeting, I got a call from the General Manager.

"Dr. Dutta, I would request you to attend the review meeting this time," he said.

Along with Mathur, I attended the meeting. During the discussions, it became quite clear to me that we have started failing in the 'Inspection and Expediting' activity. I realized that our team of inspection and expediting needed strengthening.

I assured the General Manager of BPCL that I would see to it that our team is strengthened immediately and recover any lost ground. To this I got a gem of a reply from him -

"Dr. Dutta, I called you to attend this meeting so that you get a first-hand account of where things are going wrong. I know you will take corrective actions," he said.

After a pause he continued...

"I know your organization is in a formative stage and your intentions are genuine. Let me assure you that BPCL never fails in a project and BPCL never lets its consultants and contractors fail. Take care and we shall do it right together."

What a positive statement! No blame game or fireworks. We made amends and the project moved without hiccups. It helped us fill the gaps in our organization.

It was really a pleasure to work with the BPCL team.

David versus Goliath

The other project that helped us build our organization was from Oil & Natural Gas Corporation (ONGC), for one of their oilfield production systems. It was really a David versus Goliath situation with three shortlisted bidders, our tiny Triune Projects

Private Limited and *two giant government owned companies*, Engineers India Limited (EIL) and Projects & Development India Limited (PDIL). Our bid turned out to be the lowest.

But there was a catch!

The problem was that PDIL bid was only 9% higher than our bid price. There was a discretionary rule with the Government. If the price of a government owned company was within 10% of a privately owned competitor, they could be awarded the job. The discretion lied with the Ministry of Petroleum. PDIL was pushing the Ministry to use the discretion.

Suspense! Suspense! Competition with two giants. Both determined not to let Triune, a toddler, grow up as a competitor. It was crucial to keep track of moves by all the parties involved – PDIL, our prospective client ONGC and the Ministry.

I distributed the task amongst my team members. Our marketing team was keeping liaison with lower and middle level management of ONGC. I was keeping in touch with ONGC at top management. And I put versatile Rai to find some link and make forays into the Ministry of Petroleum, which he did successfully. We used to keep each other informed of the developments daily and plan the next move.

We must have done things right. The job was awarded to us! It was our first job with a fee of 8-digit figure in Rupees with complete range of scope from concept to commissioning!

*****

Marketing Is a Team Effort

The aforementioned job was the result of an excellent team effort by a number of people. But I was surprised that almost each player in the marketing effort thought that he was the kingpin behind our success. Marketing is just like a soccer game. Someone defends an attack from the other side, someone gives an excellent forward pass and someone shoots the goal. But contribution comes from each one in the team including the coach who is not playing in the field.

When someone starts thinking that the job orders are coming due to him and he is the kingpin, it becomes a sure shot way to disaster.

THE INDISCRETIONS

Yes, it was not roses and roses all the way. I made some mistakes in our business development effort. Sometimes enthusiasm can lead to overconfidence and indiscretions. Some future maverick like me might benefit from the stories and avoid landing into similar situations.

A Glorious Entry - Then an Honorable Exit!

It was in the first few formative years of Triune. I had given my marketing people freedom to hit any order as long as it is around our core strength of design and engineering of process plants.

Our new Marketing Manager was trying hard to establish himself. Experienced in marketing of process plant hardware, he was finding it hard to get a breakthrough in marketing knowledge-based services. It was a different ball game.

He had a close contact with top management in a pharmaceutical company in Vadodara, a city known for its petrochemical and chemical industry. They were looking for an engineering consultancy company for their new project to manufacture an antibiotic, Ciprofloxacin.

"Shall I try for it?" he asked me.

By that time, I had enough confidence in my team and well organized to take up anything.

"After all it is another kind of process industry. It is the basic skill of design and engineering of process plants that matters," I thought. I gave him a go ahead.

Within a few months he succeeded in landing the job on our laps.

We celebrated it in a gathering, toasting to "An entry into the Pharmaceutical Industry." It was indeed a great breakthrough considering we had no track record in pharmaceutical industry.

But I had not foreseen the travails that would follow!

The agreement was very clear. The client would provide the basic design based on their technology. We would only convert it to a complete engineering document suitable for construction and execution of the project.

Soon the first set of basic design documents was handed over to us by our client.

Our engineering team got a shock of their life! The documents were very sketchy; drawings were hand drawn using pencil and a ruler, with very limited data and information for us to do any engineering and specifications. Alarm bells rang! To our engineers accustomed to properly drafted technology documents, it was like a bolt from the blue!

When my engineers showed the documents received from the client, I had an eerie feeling that as a budding company hungry for jobs, I made a mistake. I did not really check the capability or past record of the client to deliver the technology document as per acceptable norms and details.

We told the client that we did not have enough information to start the work.

"Don't worry," replied their manager. "We shall put our expert team in your office to guide you."

Their expert team came. The job progressed to some extent for a while, amidst a widening gap between their understanding of basic design and our understanding of the same.

Things came to a halt when we asked for the dimensions of the reactor. A reactor is an equipment where a number of raw materials can enter and react under controlled temperature and pressure conditions. In the petrochemical industry we use modeling techniques based on science and technology to size a reactor.

When asked about sizing of the reactor, their expert sitting there gave an unthinkable response! He raised his arms to shoulder level and put them apart at an obtuse angle indicating the diameter of the reactor!

"This much only. Measure the width I am showing. According to my experience, this should be the diameter of the reactor of this capacity."

That was the tipping point!

We were getting fed up with their ad-hoc approach as much as they were getting fed up with our insistence on a systematic approach. Our Project Manager rushed to my room.

"We can't take it anymore," he said. "We had celebrated our entry into the Pharmaceutical Industry. Now please do anything to get an honorable exit. We shall celebrate the exit too!"

After hard negotiations, we could settle for a reasonable compensation based on milestones completed and closed the job!

It taught us a good lesson - when venturing into an unknown area outside your knowledge domain, don't take things for granted, tread cautiously. And when a company says they will provide the technology, be sure of their capability. More so, when the company is not known as a provider of technology.

Beware of R&D Data

It was the very first year of our newly formed company. A well-known petrochemical company had developed a technology to produce food grade hexane from Naphtha.

Naphtha, a product from crude oil, is a mixture of numerous chemicals. Recovery of high purity food grade hexane from Naphtha is not easy. It is particularly difficult to eliminate benzene, a toxic chemical present in Naphtha.

The company claimed that it had been able to produce food grade hexane of right purity by distillation in their pilot plant.

Our assignment was to build a commercial scale plant based on the pilot plant data and provide all the services from design, to construction and commissioning. It was an interesting project. We succeeded in getting the order of design, engineering, project execution and commissioning of the plant.

From my past experience of a similar project in EIL, I had doubts whether hexane of such purity, almost free of benzene, could be produced just by distillation of Naphtha.

Before quoting for the job, I myself along with a colleague went to the premises of the petrochemical company to look into the pilot plant and the data produced. I looked at the pilot plant, the procedures and analytical methods etc. Every set of data on pilot plant experiments given to us showed that the product obtained by simple distillation was meeting the specifications on purity of hexane vis-a-vis benzene content.

Sometimes experimental data is fudged. But the people who carried out the studies had formidable credentials.

I had no reasons to question their integrity.

Still a lingering doubt remained in my mind based on my past knowledge. I made sure that our engineers did multiple runs in the simulation study of the process in a computer model, and checked that the product specification was comfortably met.

We designed and constructed the commercial plant based on the R&D data. But my fears turned true!

The plant designed by us could not achieve purity of hexane with respect to benzene content.

During the same period, my erstwhile company EIL was handling a very similar project of producing food grade hexane. Their R&D personnel were looking into it. I consulted them.

They had firmly concluded in their lab studies that such purity of hexane is not possible solely by simple distillation process alone. Obviously, the experimental data our client gave had some flaw somewhere.

Later, we had to solve the problem by adding a few pieces of equipment to remove the small traces of benzene from hexane. But we faced a lot of flak from the client and our reputation took a beating.

Where did I commit a mistake? I violated an advice by my superior Krishnamurthy during my tenure with EIL

"Never trust experimental data for a new technology to do a scaled-up design of a commercial plant," he had advised me.

"It is not just the probability of a fudged data," he said. "There could be a probability of some unintentional errors even when the data is generated by able and sincere scientists and engineers. There could be errors in some of the procedures adopted during conducting the studies, like error in the calibration of high-tech instruments used for analysis of products."

I still remember the advice he gave me.

"Before accepting the data, ask the client to do a complete run of experiments in their prototype or pilot plant, in presence of reliable experts engaged by you, checking each and every detail."

Why didn't I do it? As a small budding company, we did not have the resources to carry out such an investigation.

Did I get swayed by the enthusiasm of executing a challenging project for a well-known company in the very first year of our existence? Or because of the formidable credentials of the people who were behind the experimental studies by the client?

I cannot vouch that, if I were to time travel to the past to exactly the same situation, I would have taken a different decision.

It is always good to learn, make the best of the present time and move forward in spite of some mistakes and indiscretions.

*****

------------ *The Art of Living in The Present*----------------

In this context, I can't help recalling an interview I saw in TV. Sunil Gavaskar, the legendary cricket player of India was being interviewed. He used to play for India in the 1970s, when The West Indies were the strongest cricket team in the world. They had some of the fastest and fiercest bowlers in the world. And those days protective armors like modern helmets and paddings were not so developed. Sunil Gavaskar, in his first appearance for India against West Indies, showed exemplary skill and concentration as opening batsman and scored hundreds of runs in almost all the matches.

The interviewer on the TV asked him, "How do you keep so much concentration ball after ball? Sometimes when you play some shots wrong, don't you get irritated and lose concentration?"

"Maybe for a moment," he replied. "But immediately I get ready to face the next ball. And at that moment all that matters to me is to face the six plus feet tall and hostile bowler running towards the wicket to hurl the ball at over 90 miles per hour to me. Nothing else in the world matters at that point of time."

TOWARDS ADULTHOOD – 1994 TO 1996

Overseas Forays

Jacob had registered a small marketing outpost in Singapore with the same name – Triune Projects Pvt. Ltd. during the very first year of starting. He appointed Menon, a professional with smart and suave demeanor, to take charge of the Singapore office.

Mathur and I along with Jacob made our first marketing blitz for the South East Asian market. Our objective was to get engineering work offloaded to our Delhi office. Menon had very systematically organized a schedule of meetings with some major companies in Singapore. But we were a company of too small a size at that stage. The visit eventually resulted in some opportunities for placement of engineers in some Singapore companies.

We had no intention to get into the business of manpower supply. *Our aim was to get orders offloaded to our Delhi office.*

As manpower placement opportunities built up, we met the requirements by appointing engineers of high caliber as full-time employees of Triune, not on contract basis for placement.

This helped us build the manpower base in Triune with good engineers to meet the need of future business, besides improving cash flow for growth. It also helped us build relationships with overseas companies.

Some significant events took place with both positive and negative impact at this stage. But before we come to that, here is break with an interesting anecdote.

*****

-------------The Art of Understanding People---------------

Jacob had announced the appointment of Menon in one of our management meetings. He circulated the appointment letter for Menon to us for any comments. It was a formal appointment letter prepared by Jacob himself very professionally, with job description, his role, functions and responsibilities, compensation, terms and conditions all explained in detail.

"Hey, you never gave me a letter of agreement like that when I joined?" looking at it I commented.

Jacob gave an interesting reply.

"Utpal, with your style of functioning of treading into undefined paths and creating your own role, had I given you a similar letter, you wouldn't have been able to function at all!"

When I told this to my wife after returning home, she smiled and commented, "He really understands people. He has understood you perfectly."

The art of understanding people is one of the key elements of success.

The Assault on Triune

The Central Bureau of Investigation (CBI) was set up as the premier investigating agency of India, with the noble idea of fighting corruption. But under the government of India, it was often misused to serve the interests of those in power in the central government. Gopal Krishna Gandhi, an eminent diplomat of India commented, "The CBI is seen as Government's hatchet, rather than honesty's ally."

One morning we were surprised to hear that CBI had called Jacob for interrogation in connection with something. Later CBI kept him in their custody for questioning for indefinite period and slapped some charges against him in the court.

Knowing Jacob well, I was totally confident that he could not have done anything wrong that violates the law of the land in any way. I knew he would be back with us, stronger than ever and clean, after grilling by CBI and their lawyers. And it exactly happened that way eventually.

But in the interim period, from the day he was taken in by CBI and for the next few days I had to weather a severe storm. The news spread like wildfire in the industry.

"Triune is finished," some jealous competitors spread the word in the market.

I got a number of anxious calls from our clients asking me if our office was working. One of our clients who offloaded quite a bit of work on us, even offered me to join their company with my entire team. They were worried that their projects might suffer.

To all of them, I gave the same reply in a calm but firm voice, somewhat like this –

"There are absolutely no charges by CBI against Triune Projects Private Limited, which I run. There could be some malicious charges related to one of Jacob's other companies which will blow off soon. As far as Triune Projects Private Limited is concerned, I am the owner and in full control of the company. We all are hale and hearty here. Your jobs are in safe hands."

It was absolutely audacious of a miniscule stake-holder like me to claim to be the owner!

The crisis situation made me respond in a very authentic and convincing way. Within a short time, peace prevailed - all quiet, business as usual.

Sometimes telling the truth but not the whole truth for the benefit of all is fine!

As for Jacob, he came out stronger and more confident, cleared by the court of all charges!

Back to office, he must have been pleased to see things under control, with Mathur and I moving around in Russia, for an attractive business prospect.

From Russia – A Masterclass in Marketing

Both Mathur and I were keeping in touch with our network of friends around the world.

One such contact was our ex-colleagues, Sarin, of the same EIL breed. He was running a small engineering services company in the USA. He had excellent business contacts in Russia.

One day, in December 1994, I got a very interesting fax message from Sarin! I don't remember the words exactly, but it was something like this…

"We are about to sign an agreement to execute a major project in Russia. Please come with your key management personnel and heads of engineering departments to Moscow by next weekend. We may sign the contract and have a project kick-off meeting during the visit."

Though a very exciting message, Mathur and I decided it was too optimistic. It was unthinkable that in one shot all agreements would be signed and a project kick-off meeting would take place. The risk of taking a big team to Russia was financially too much for our budding company.

We were confident that between the two of us we would be able to handle any situation that might arise out of the meeting.

Few would love to travel to Russia in the midst of cold winter. Moreover, Russia, under a political and economic transition in the mid-nineties, was not a recommended place to visit. But both of us were thrilled with the prospect of facing the unknown in totally alien circumstances.

We landed at Moscow International Airport in a brutally cold afternoon. The whole city looked dazzling white with a thick layer of snow. We were received at the airport by Ivan, who was Sarin's Russian associate. We were taken straight to his office-cum-guesthouse.

We rested for a while before going for an overnight journey by train to Dzerzhinsk, a petrochemical center 450 kilometers away from Moscow. Tired after a long flight, Sushil and I fell asleep soon after boarding the train.

Ivan woke us up around 6.00 AM and told us that we were nearing our destination. I opened the window curtains and could see the spread of white snow all around, shining with reflected colors of the rising sun.

We got down as the train stopped and were taken to a hotel. Soon after completing the morning rituals, I got a call from Ivan.

"Breakfast is ready. The General Manager of the Petrochemical Company, our client, is hosting the breakfast."

As we entered the dining hall, what a surprise! What a surprise!

Dr.Dravid, a friend of mine and CEO of a major engineering company in India, then known as Humphreys & Glasgow Limited, greeted us. We found that he had come with his team of four experts on an exactly similar message from Sarin.

Also present was Sarin with his team of four or five people senior professionals, which was perhaps his entire staff!

Soon we realized that it was a *master stroke* of marketing by Sarin! He managed to gather a number of top-notch professionals with decades of experience as part of his team.

The client's side too had a team of similar number for breakfast. It was a lavish breakfast spread on a long table.

In front of each of us there was a small Vodka bottle – my first experience of toasting with Vodka or for that matter any drink, during a breakfast meet!

Though apprehensive in the beginning, I found it to be a useful accompaniment to face the Russian cold.

At around 10.00 AM we were taken to a conference room in our Russian client's office. Sarin introduced each of us as his team member presenting our background. It was followed by a convincing presentation by Sarin on how he was going to execute the project.

It was a sizable project. I couldn't help appreciating Sarin's marketing skill. With a very small outfit of his own, he presented a formidable team of professionals, which looked capable enough to execute the project. And he did not spend anything beyond the expenses of his own team of five people.

It was an exemplary demo of business development!

It demonstrated that as long as you have a credible face and capability to garner resources, you can pick up big jobs.

The end result? Yes, Sarin's company got the contract, and offloaded a relatively small but high-end part of the job to Triune.

It was the first of high-end basic design jobs, offloaded to our home office in India from an overseas client!

*****

RISE AND FALL IN FORTUNES

Going Great and Rising Fortunes

By around 1994-95 things were going great for Triune. There were good ongoing projects and good fund flow from overseas placements.

But we did not want to be in the manpower placement business. One of our prime objectives, an engineering order directly offloaded on our home office from overseas, was still eluding us.

We touched the total strength of the company to over 100 technical personnel. Our finance looked healthy. At this stage, a substantial amount of surplus fund was generated for the first time since our operation. There was almost 100% utilization of manpower on jobs.

We had established ourselves as a credible engineering company in both domestic and international market. Now there was a need for a quantum jump to a bigger league.

With surplus fund now, I put all my focus for the quantum jump into turnover of 9-digit value in Rupees. That required a jump also in the consultancy orders of 9-digit value!

Mathur was focusing on his contacts with Hyundai and other overseas contractors with a sizable overseas job in the horizon.

I started focusing on large Indian projects. Soon we landed into good possibilities of two major Indian refinery projects. An interesting story on it follows in the next episode.

I was hoping at least one of the three opportunities including one from Hyundai, Korea would materialize.

The Sudden Fall

In the 1990s, the developed world had become very conscious about the adverse impact of environmental pollution on the earth. That opened up the possibility of an enormous opportunity.

The Intergovernmental Panel on Climate Change, established by the United Nations firmly pronounced the long-term effects of global warming would be dramatic and disastrous for mankind.

At that point, a number of changes were created in the specification of petroleum products to drastically reduce the harmful emissions. Particularly so, for emission due to benzene and sulfur compounds present in petroleum products. The USA as the largest consumer of petroleum products, took the first initiatives.

To meet the stringent specifications created for the products like motor gasoline, diesel etc., the existing refineries in the USA had to make huge investments, with no matching benefit in prices. As a result, many old refineries in the USA and other countries built with billions of dollars investment announced closure and sale of the refinery on *"as is where is"* basis.

And the price? Often a few million dollars only!

This opened a window of opportunity for us. A number of entrepreneurs in India and other Asian countries, where environment related specifications were far less stringent, wanted to buy those refineries and relocate. We got a number of orders for feasibility studies for relocating them in India.

Many of them, not familiar with the complexity of a refinery installation, had a misconception.

They thought it was just shifting of some equipment from one place to another. Getting something costing billions of dollars at a price of few million dollars appeared very attractive to them.

Relocation of a complex refinery has numerous cost components. It involves inspection and recovering hundreds of retrievable equipment from the old refineries, transporting, refurbishing of the equipment recovered, buying the unrecoverable parts of the refinery. It also involved re-engineering for a new location and reinstalling under totally different weather and soil conditions.

Our feasibility study estimates showed that it would cost around 85% of the investment required for a totally new refinery!

That separated the men from the boys. The novices looking for a quick profit walked out.

Two companies, very large business houses in India familiar with projects involving billions of dollars, remained in the fray. One of them was the Vedant Group, worth billions of dollars. The other was from the famous billionaire group of the Jindal family.

Both knew that for a refinery that may cost 10 billion dollars as a brand-new installation, getting it for 8.5 billion dollars gives them a substantial competitive advantage. The owners personally got involved and called us for meetings, which Jacob, Mathur and I attended together. They gave a work order to Triune to prepare a detailed project report, to get approval and license from the Government of India and then raise the finance.

They even called for quotations from us and other engineering consultants for the entire range of consultancy services for relocation. They were almost ready to start the work the moment approval from the government was received.

And we turned out to be the lowest bidder for the consultancy services! The value of the job to us was in 9 digits in Rupees, big enough for a quantum jump. The job appeared to be almost in our hands.

I always used to tell people that however prospective an opportunity may look, don't depend on it till you receive a letter of order and advance payment to start the work.

But hobnobbing with two major industrialists and seeing their personal interest, even I thought it was almost on our laps.

But abruptly the prospects vanished, like a mirage!

Approval from the government did not come through! I do not know the exact reasons. One explanation given was that the powers that be, might have killed the project. In India as in many other countries, there are influencers and lobbies to protect their interest. It was perhaps one of them.

The pursuit of the two large projects for quantum jump had taken my attention away from prospects of a number of small projects which had been keeping our funds flowing. I had put a lot of my time and resources behind the pursuit of those large path breaking projects.

Suddenly the surplus we had generated started vanishing. It was a dip in fortunes. I always prided myself on being optimistic and positive in attitude. For once I became a bit worried.

At this point I felt Jacob also became quite unhappy about depletion of the surplus reserves.

A Silver Lining in The Sky

The only immediate possibility in the horizon for a step jump was a project on a Floating Production, Storage and Offloading system (normally known as FPSO) from Hyundai Heavy Industries of Korea. They had got a contract to build it for a Brazilian Oil Company. They were looking for engineering consultancy services for the project.

A lot depended now on Mathur's effort to get the order from Hyundai Heavy Industries for engineering of the FPSO production facilities.

The project if it materialized, would lead us to path breaking area of offshore production technology. It was the cutting-edge technology in oil and gas production those days. Mathur's efforts were progressing well.

Mathur seemed to be zeroing in towards the job order.

In the next few months, certain events moved rapidly that took Triune to another level.

*****

------------------- *Layman's Guide to FPSO* -------------------

Floating Production, Storage & Offloading system (FPSO) is a popular concept in deep sea, over 500 meters in depth, where it is uneconomical to build the production platforms supported by structures fixed on sea bed.

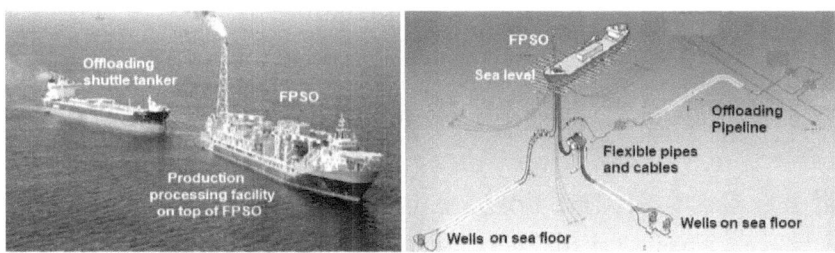

The photograph on the left shows an FPSO. All the production and processing facilities are built on top of a large oil tanker with a deck size of a few hundred meters in length and fifty-sixty meters in width. It anchors at an oilfield location in the deep sea.

*The sketch at right shows how oil wells drilled on sea floor going deep down, are connected to the facilities on the tanker with flexible piping. The hull of the tanker acts as a large storage. Crude oil is **offloaded** from the storage either by a shuttle tanker as shown in the left picture. Or by a pipeline laid on the sea floor as shown in the sketch on right.*

It was a cutting-edge technology in production of oil and natural gas from oilfields lying below deep sea, 2000 meters or more. For engineering consultants like Triune, the role is to execute design and engineering of the complex production and processing facilities on top of the FPSO.

THE METAMORPHOSIS (1995 – 1997)

Restructuring the Company

Since 1993, Jacob and I felt that with the business and size of the company growing, we needed a board with well-known professionals as members and a full-time chairman to guide the company. He had in mind a prominent technocrat, ex-chairman of a major IT company in India. I had some difference of opinion on the selection of the Chairman.

I discussed the matter with my colleague Basu. Both of us felt that the Chairman of Triune should be from the Oil & Natural Gas industry. Both of us ultimately converged on P.K. Rudra, an outstanding technocrat in the oil and gas industry.

Rudra had grown from grass root level to top echelons of quite a few major companies in India. Both Basu and I had known him when he was working in Engineers India Limited (EIL) during our tenure there. After leaving EIL, he rose to the level of Chairman and Managing Director of two major companies. Later he was back to EIL as the Chairman and Managing Director. He had retired from EIL at that point of time.

We proposed Rudra's name to Jacob. He too was familiar with Rudra's profile and was very open to it.

My last interaction with Rudra had been in one of my forays to EIL in search of people. I recall once he came out of his office and happened to see me. He saw me sitting with one of the executives. I greeted him.

He immediately pointed his finger to me and said something like, "Hey! He has snatched a few senior people from our company."

It was not a rude expression though not a very approving one. That's how he always was, blunt and straight talking, with no hard feelings.

We decided that the best person to approach him would be Basu, a senior and well-respected person in the industry, in the same genre as Rudra. It was decided that based on Rudra's response to Basu, Jacob would meet him. Rudra's response was positive.

Meeting between Jacob and Rudra went well. Soon Rudra joined as full-time Chairman of the company.

Meanwhile, Mathur had zeroed in on the Hyundai FPSO job. A call from them was expected any day. It had reached a stage where a draft contract was getting ready for discussion with Hyundai.

Vanishing From The Scene

The eagerly anticipated call from Hyundai for discussion on the contract for their FPSO project came at last! Hyundai had selected a Chinese shipyard for fabrication of the floating system. Their management team was in Beijing finalizing the deal with them. They called us to come to Beijing to finalize our contract.

Mathur had minor illness at the time. We decided that Rai, our commercial man, and I would travel to China to negotiate and sign the contract for engineering of a major floating production (FPSO).

Rai and I landed in Beijing on a bright and sunny morning with great anticipation and checked in at Holiday Inn, Beijing.

After settling down in our rooms and a refreshing bath, we were ready to meet the client for negotiation. There were frequent calls from the home office at New Delhi. All waiting in anticipation!

The contract document was created earlier by Hyundai. We had some time to look through the documents. The next day after eight hours of tedious discussions, all points were agreed upon, our fee was settled and the contract was ready.

The moment we signed the contract, it gave us the feeling of a great relief and immense happiness!

Ours was a small start-up company and the order value was a game changer for us. It was more than our annual turnover. We had agreed to create a separate 100-man task force exclusively committed to the Hyundai project.

Just imagine! Our total strength at that time was around 100 plus technical people.

It meant doubling our capacity within a few months!

Moreover, for Triune it was entering into cutting edge technology of deep-sea oil and gas production, which no other company in India at that point of time had entered into.

At last, we had reached a state where we were about to jump into a major league of international engineering consultancy companies.

We knew the moment we sent the news to our home office in Delhi, we would be flooded with numerous calls and action plans. As CEO of the company, I took the liberty to spend one peaceful day in Beijing, as a reward to ourselves.

I sent a cryptic message to our office. It was something like -

"Pole star is shining bright! We are vanishing from the scene."

Rai and I switched off our phones. Then we quietly checked out of the hotel and checked into another hotel, without informing anyone, except our families.

The Impact of Hyundai's FPSO Order

As an engineering consultancy company, we sold knowledge-based services. The value of an order depends on how many technical people are needed for what period of time. The implications of the Hyundai order to Triune were momentous.

Firstly, as I mentioned we had to double our manpower capacity. Along with that came the task of quickly acquiring more office space and infrastructure!

Secondly, it was an entry of Triune into the frontier technology area of engineering of deep-sea production on a floating facility. It required addition of people of high caliber with relevant experience.

Challenging international project orders draw good professionals. Credible management also draws good professionals. We had both at this point of time.

There was a rush of excellent engineers joining us at that point. The real challenge was managing smooth induction of so many employees with adequate office space and infrastructure. We did rise to the occasion.

But there was one collateral damage. Attention of management and everyone got diverted to the Hyundai FPSO project. Besides large workload in Delhi office, it also had substantial work at Hyundai's Korea office and at work site in China in our scope. That created numerous opportunities for overseas postings.

Almost all engineers working for long with us thought they should get the first chance of getting into the project!

As a result, many of the ongoing smaller jobs which helped to sustain our growth suffered. That created some adverse impact on our image and goodwill with some of our Indian clients.

Starting with a Bang

I am not talking about starting of Hyundai FPSO project. This is about Rudra, our new full-time Chairman. While I knew him since long, it was my first experience of working with him.

We had developed our organization structure, systems and procedures. But there were lacunae which we used to overcome with personal heroics and fire-fighting.

With his formidable background in management, Rudra was the right man at the right time. He started with a bang from the very first day going about 'settings things right'. Yes, setting things right in systems, procedures, project execution pitfalls and organization.

His contribution to Triune in this tumultuous period was of immense value.

But while God had given him so many attributes of a top-notch management person, he had one contrarian aspect in his persona. It was his lack of humility.

I would be surprised if Rudra raises any objection when he reads this. Because he was actually proud of this aspect of his persona. Often after delivering stories of his achievements, he would look at the audience for any reaction and happily announce, "I am not a person known for humility."

Jim Collins in his book "Good to Great" analyzed common traits of great leaders. "These leaders are paradoxical blend of personal humility and professional will," he observed. "They are more like Lincoln and Socrates than Patton and Caesar."

A Glance at the Future

"The only way to do great work is to do what you love to do."

~ Steve Jobs

I worked closely with Rudra and developed a working relationship of mutual respect, though in many ways we were quite apart in our approach. Soon the board was restructured with a few prominent technocrats from the industry as external Directors on the board. Procedures for board meetings and approvals were set in a very professional manner. Work process and systems were well set.

It was interesting for a while. But accustomed to working with complete freedom for past several years, I started sensing that I am weaving a chrysalis around myself.

I felt that it was hindering my normal way of functioning. Some urge for a change started creeping in my mind at this stage.

Or would I prefer a life that churns and puts me into new adventures of doing something for the first time again?

I started visualizing how I would like to see my life in future.

"In peace I rest. In chaos I thrive."

*****

THE TURNING POINT

The Trigger

> *"The graveyards are full of indispensable people."*
>
> ~ *Charles De Gaulle*

At certain point of time, Mathur became the key anchor in the overseas business development effort. He was a very much known face to the Korean and international contractors. Besides Hyundai, his contact helped us get some smaller jobs from Daewoo and Samsung of Korea too.

Mathur's closeness and bonhomie with the Korean companies was an asset to the company. But his becoming indispensable to Triune was a concern.

Not that I had any lack of trust in him. But even the most committed people do change jobs.

I happen to be a strong believer in the axiom *that someone's indispensability is a double whammy*. It halts personal growth of the person and it creates a situation for potential disaster for the company. As a first step, I had made sure that I was dispensable to Triune by creating a formidable top management.

To create alternative access to the overseas companies, I had placed Rai to follow up and interact on Korean jobs from Daewoo and Samsung. He developed reasonable rapport and credibility with Daewoo and Samsung in a short period.

Also, I was eager to create an alternative to Mathur by inducting someone equally known to the overseas companies.

In this context I recall an event which triggered my urge for exit from Triune.

A few months prior to the award of the contract from

Hyundai, an important meeting was called by the Hyundai management in Korea. Mathur was invited by them to attend the meeting. With the idea of developing another contact point with Hyundai, I put Rai to accompany him.

After Rudra joined, he had a number of interactions with Jacob and other members of management team including me.

I was taken aback by one comment Rudra made during one of our interactions.

"I am quite surprised that Jacob raised question on your decision to send Rai along with Mathur for a meeting in Korea," he said.

"It was thought by him to be an unnecessary expenditure," he continued. "I fully supported your decision. I think it was the right thing to do," he concluded.

This became the first trigger for my own metamorphosis. Not that I grudged anyone questioning me. But as a person leading the company, I wished the question was put to me directly.

Though looking back, I feel it was a small thing, but under the circumstances it was the final trigger.

I recalled Jacob's comment when I had asked him why did he not create a formal letter of agreement with me when I joined, like he did for others.

His reply was, *"Utpal, with your style of functioning of treading into undefined paths and creating your own role, had I given you a similar letter, you wouldn't have been able to function at all!"*

To break out of the cocoon I was building around myself and fly out, became an irresistible urge.

I had an interesting interaction with Rai at this stage. I was telling him that the time for my exit has come.

"But Binoy trusts and depends a lot on you," he replied, surprised.

"Yes," I said, "he trusts me completely. But due to certain recent events, I feel his confidence in me is diminished."

"There is a difference between trust and confidence." I added.

The Path to Exit

There were possibilities of my moving to another similar company. But I had realized that I wanted the life of a free bird, not a caged one. A plan was brewing in my mind to start a small consultancy firm of my own focusing on niche areas.

I had a number of sittings with Jacob and Rudra on my intent for a change. Meanwhile Rajiv, who was heading the Triune Singapore outfit, expressed his desire to quit and submitted his resignation.

We all finally agreed that instead of leaving Triune, I would take charge of Triune Singapore office to create opportunities for Triune in the international market. I liked the idea.

First, I felt confident that I could create the Singapore outpost as a base for flow of overseas jobs. That would serve for one unfinished task of mine. It would serve my purpose of creating an alternative to the flow of overseas jobs from Mathur's personal contacts alone.

Second, at that time a very important criteria for me, the posting at Singapore at that level of remuneration would make me financially more stable.

Though, it pushed back my urge to create an entity of my own, a step which I was determined to take sooner or later.

After having sent numerous engineers working with me both in Engineers India Limited and Triune on lucrative long-term foreign assignments, it was my own first long-term foreign assignment. By age, I was in the later half of fifties at that time. But it was worth the wait because I never wanted a routine foreign assignment.

Singapore was another kind of challenge – carving out a new door for Triune to enter the overseas market. And it was a transition in continuity with Triune India before exit, rather than an abrupt exit. I started looking forward to it.

I suggested to Rudra and Jacob that Mathur should be my successor as CEO, which was readily accepted. It was immensely satisfying that I would be leaving behind a strong and well-structured management team.

Sometime in 1997, I joined Triune Singapore office.

On my relocation from Triune India to Triune Singapore, I was given a sentimental farewell and gifts from my colleagues. Jacob issued a notification in recognition of my contribution towards Triune, which was a very gratifying parting gift.

The notification, full of praise and appreciation, was something I really did not ask for or looked forward to. I normally shrug off both praise or criticism in profession as routine professional hazards.

But frankly I liked and relished the way Jacob put it. That is because I knew it came out genuinely from his heart. Also, because certain passages matched with my own perception about myself. I am taking the liberty of putting certain parts from the notification here as closure of this chapter.

A Salute to Dr. U. K. Dutta

"Utpal Dutta's contribution to making Triune what it is today cannot be overstated – 260 staff, significant infrastructure, market penetration in major industry segments. Rarely has something so significant been created in such a short time..........

"As he always says, he is a dreamer. He has noble and ambitious dreams. What is admirable is the tenacity and commitment he has to make his vision a reality. He has always tried to make people around him share his dreams and work towards achieving them. It is a compliment to his nobility that when any of his team members failed, he stood up to the firing line to take the blame.

CHAPTER - 4

BREAKING BARRIERS IN SINGAPORE

START AFRESH IN A NEW ENVIRONMENT

Sometime in 1997, I landed in Singapore to start a stimulating and at the same time a testing phase of my career. Mission - *to establish the Singapore office as source of overseas orders for the Triune home office in Delhi.*

Singapore is one of those rare places where everything worked perfectly. A bit too strictly, but with precision. Add to that, it was known as the most business friendly government the world over.

I started there in the period of economic slump in South East Asia from 1997 to 1999. When there were some signs of economic recovery, there came one of the worst oil price slumps, crude oil prices falling close to US$ 10/ barrel around 1999.

In the challenging market situation, I targeted at least one order of large value per year to start with. I resorted to the best way I knew to start business development – meet personal contacts and expand the network.

I soon got an interesting lead for a major opportunity in Vietnam. I went all out for it! It was a unique battle for me – *The Battle of Vietnam!*

*****

THE BATTLE OF VIETNAM

(Note: All the names of characters and companies in the narrative have been changed due to confidentiality)

Getting Battle-ready

I got a lead from someone that Pet-Viet, a company owned by the government of Vietnam, had issued an enquiry for consultancy to build a large LPG Terminal in Vietnam.

"Be careful," someone experienced in the Vietnam business environment cautioned me.

"Vietnam is not Singapore," he said. "There could be a lot of obstacles and foul play. Better engage an agent with good penetration in Vietnam to hand-hold you in that market."

Immediately, I started a search for a right agency in Singapore to represent Triune in Vietnam. After scrutinizing some, I soon zeroed in on a company CP Agency. It was owned by a guy called Cheng Peng.

I met Cheng Peng and discussed the matter with him in detail within a span of a few days. He briefed me which companies he represented in Vietnam and what all he had done for them. He had represented an Indian hardware company with reasonable success in Vietnam. After the discussions, I felt confident he knew the Vietnam business environment quite well.

I asked Cheng Peng what his strength was with the Pet-Viet Limited, who were our potential client.

"I know the Head of Finance in the company quite well. I had successful business interactions with him in connection with another project," he replied.

His reply added to my confidence. In Vietnam under communist regime, all major companies were owned by the

Government. Having dealt with government owned companies in India, I knew of the enormous powers the finance man wields in such companies.

I signed an agreement with CP Agency to represent us in Vietnam. Subsequently, Cheng Peng gave me some papers on the project.

"These are enquiry documents on the project," he briefed me. "Bechtel of USA is going to be your main competitor. They are favorites with Pet-Viet management."

"When is the bid due?" I asked.

"The bid is due in one week. But don't worry," he replied. "I have first-hand information that they will extend the bid submission date. Get ready with a draft proposal and visit Vietnam."

"I have an office there," he continued. "My man Dung will meet you at your hotel and arrange a meeting with a key management person of Pet-Viet Ltd. You can totally trust Dung."

"You can review your draft bid with my contact in Pet-Viet and tell him how much time you need to prepare your bid," added Cheng Peng.

Little did I realize that this would set me up for a series of adventures, in Vietnam, of a kind I had not bargained for!

An Encounter of the Third Kind

One-week time was too short a time for our tiny Singapore office to prepare a proposal. Deepali, my wife, lent a helping hand and we somehow could put together a draft proposal. We both landed in Ho Chi Minh city (*Saigon*) one morning and checked into the Plaza Hotel.

Dung, a colleague of Cheng Peng in Vietnam, soon contacted me and dropped in. He was a young Vietnamese local, quite friendly in disposition. After some pleasantries, Dung made some statements which sounded quite alarming!

"Be careful of what you say in public. You are a foreigner. Very often foreigners, particularly first-time visitors like you, are tracked by the police. Even walls have ears here. If they get any doubt, your phones might be tapped," Dung warned.

"This enquiry document from Pet-Viet is for an important project and of a fairly high value," he continued. "Secret agencies in Vietnam may track you, once they know you have come for business. We shall arrange all meetings outside, not in Pet-Viet office."

What he said next was equally alarming.

"I shall call my contact in Pet-Viet from a safe location outside the hotel," he said. "Depending on the time he gives for a meeting, I shall send a message to you to see me outside the hotel."

He left, giving me a sense of an imminent adventure!

At around 5 PM Dung sent me a message to come out of the hotel. He spotted me as I came out. He hired a cab and mentioned the destination to the cab driver in Vietnamese language.

The taxi crisscrossed through some streets and alleys. The environment around was totally alien to me. We reached a two storied building. Dung paid the cab driver. At the gate there were a few sturdy people in smart black dress who looked like bouncers. Dung told them something which allowed our entry into the building.

I immediately noticed something quite unusual for me! All around there were a number of very beautiful girls in pink dresses. There were no outsiders at that time except Dung and I. Sensing my discomfort, Dung explained that customers would start coming in the evening!

One of the pretty girls showed us to a small meeting room with a longish table with chairs around. Dung ordered some beer.

"The man I am going to introduce you to, loves beer," Dung explained.

Soon another pretty girl entered with a trolley. I was surprised to see at least two dozen of beer cans placed on our table. I thought quite a few people would be there in the meeting.

After some wait, a middle-aged gentleman was ushered into the room. Dung completed the formalities of introduction. He was Nguyen, Head of Finance in Pet-Viet Ltd.

Dung and Nguyen started discussing something between them in Vietnamese. It was quite intense and lasted for a fairly long time. It ended with Nguyen extending his hand towards me and started a conversation with me in pure English.

"Dung is a friend and we trust each other," he said. "Dung has convinced me that I can trust you and your company. We are friends now."

I shook hands with him and confirmed, "Yes, you can trust me."

Beer cans were opened. I found both Dung and Nguyen were consuming the beer cans at a rate much faster than I have ever seen. By the time I was consuming one can, they were consuming three to four cans each. The meeting lasted two hours roughly from 6 PM to 8 PM. All of the two dozen of beer cans and some more were consumed between the three of us.

The meeting brought out a lot of clarity. Nguyen was Head of Finance and a key member of a team nominated by Pet-Viet to evaluate the bids.

"I have asked for a re-bid," he announced. "You shall get more than a month's time to prepare and submit your bid."

He took a quick glance through our draft bid document. He explained to me their internal procedures for bid evaluation, the evaluation criteria and tips on how to meet the criteria. He even handed over some internal documents related to their bid evaluation method. Then he briefed me on some "Dos" and "Don'ts" on preparation of the bids.

"Bechtel of USA has dug deep in our company. They are favorites with majority in the bid evaluation team. Make a perfect bid and give me a competitive price, and the job will be yours," Nguyen stated confidently.

He also gave some idea on the price Bechtel was likely to quote.

Then came a surprise! Three young and gorgeous girls in min-skirts came in, greeted us and ushered us into a private dining room! Each of us had one girl sitting next to us!

Next to me was a beautiful and sophisticated young girl in mini-skirt, starting a conversation with me in good English. The others were speaking in Vietnamese. She turned out to be working as a secretary in some company.

With drinks served and music on, people started cozying up to each other. The environment with the potential threat of some secret agency tracking us and beautiful girls all around, was something like a scene straight from a James Bond movie.

But not being a James Bond kind of personality, I started feeling distinctly uncomfortable within!

I managed to maintain a worldly-wise exterior. My mini-skirted girl companion almost started rubbing her bare thighs with mine. Unaccustomed to such niceties, I thought it was time for me to exit.

I made a very brief announcement appreciating the beautiful environment and charming girls around. I concluded with the statement that my wife who had accompanied me in Saigon was waiting for dinner with me in the hotel, and Dung would ensure that they all have a great time.

"See you again soon," said Nguyen, our key contact in Pet-Viet. I waved at him and was relieved to make a quick exit.

On return to Singapore, I described the events and my discomfiture to Rajiv, my predecessor. He had a hearty laugh.

"This is quite common in business dealings in some parts of the Far-East. Having a female escort with you is an accepted business norm. Be prepared for such situations," he advised.

"But be careful," he advised. "People are known to vanish there, if under suspicion."

----------------An Encounter of The Third Kind--------------

The title of the preceding episode 'An Encounter of the Third Kind' may surprise some. This kind of expression commonly relates to encounters with Unidentified Flying Objects (UFO).

Encounters with UFO have been categorized into five kinds.

The first kind is sighting one within a short distance.

The second kind is a UFO sighting with a physical effect like interference in the functioning of a vehicle or electronic device, or paralysis or heat and discomfort in the witness.

The third kind is an encounter and interaction with visible aliens in a UFO. It could be a robot or some kind of alien living being.

The fourth kind is being taken in by the aliens and having undergone experiment by the aliens.

The fifth kind is direct communication and relationship with aliens.

My first encounter in Vietnam was limited to the third kind. I had managed to escape from the fourth kind of encounter!

The Battle for the Contract

Soon, we received the invitation to bid for the project from Pet-Viet. I sent it immediately to Triune India office. I was quite thrilled at the impending battle in an international arena.

I sent all the feedback that Nguyen gave me to Triune home office in India. Our bid was submitted in due time.

The battlegrounds were open. I had to make at least four or five visits to Vietnam for follow up till concluding of the contract. But I was careful to avoid encounters of the third kind as far as possible.

Cheng Peng got feedback that a few members of Pet-Viet were trying hard to disqualify Triune. But we had met all the evaluation criteria given by Nguyen. Soon we were invited by Pet-Viet for a meeting to discuss the technical part of our bid. Rai from India and I attended the meeting.

Mr. Hong, Head of their Engineering Department in Pet-Viet called us for the meeting. He seemed to be openly hostile.

He expressed grave doubts about our office infrastructure in India.

"We are executing a big project of Hyundai Heavy Industries from our office," I replied. "Their engineers are sitting in our office and have no complaints about our infrastructure. You are welcome to visit our office and see for yourself. We shall be glad to host you there."

He cooled down. I surmised that perhaps the prospect of a potential overseas trip pacified him a bit.

"But why don't you do some part of the work like basic design in Singapore," he insisted.

The prospect of a deputation of their technical team in a place like Singapore was obviously tempting.

"This can give your company an opportunity to start a *design engineering hub* at Singapore. Think about it," Cheng Peng whispered in my ears.

I thought about it. Firstly, Singapore was so far planned as an *outpost* rather than a *hub*. Also, our proposal was not prepared on those lines. I surmised that from a winning position, it was better to pursue our proposal as it was, rather than a sudden change of the goal post.

I knew of enormous effort and resources required for a start-up venture like Triune India. I had no appetite for repeating the feat.

I insisted on going along as per our proposal.

He took another angle of attack. He asked us to submit within a day, detailed profile of all our lead engineers of every discipline who would work for the project. We got the response from Triune India promptly and submitted it well in time.

The response from India had a list of some of our best engineers with excellent credentials. But the way we Indians love to have venerable designations rather than functional ones, created a major hassle, with a threat from Hong to disqualify us.

Eventually we were cleared on technical evaluation. Now it was the time for opening the prices and final decision by **the client!**

--------- The Hazards of Venerable Designations---------

In the last para, I mentioned 'a major hassle'. It emanated from an archaic culture in India that reveres managerial designations more than functional designation based on role and specialization.

All over the world, the technical personnel working in engineering consultancy companies are designated according to their level and function. Designations like Mechanical Design Engineer, Scientist Level 1, Lead Electrical Engineer, Principal Consultant, Senior Metallurgist etc. are commonly used and respected. But in India, a manager, irrespective of his responsibilities, is socially more revered than a top-notch specialist. Designations are given accordingly.

In the list of our key personnel submitted to Pet-Viet, most engineers were designated as Manager, Senior Manager, Chief Manager etc. Hong, the Chief Engineer of Pet-Viet, jumped at us after seeing the list.

"What shall we do with so many managers?" he stated. "You have no working engineers in the team. We are going to disqualify you."

We had quite a bit of explaining to do verbally and in writing to avoid disqualification. We even had to do a bit of explaining to a senior management person of the parent company (holding company) of Pet-Viet, whose support Cheng Peng had garnered.

The Final Encounter (of The Third kind)

One fine morning in Singapore I got a call from Cheng Peng that Nguyen, our friend in Pet-Viet wanted to meet me at Saigon on a certain date.

"He wants to give me some very important confidential message," said Cheng Peng.

I was also advised to bring some expensive gift for Nguyen.

I immediately sent a message to Rai to reach Saigon. This time too Cheng Peng himself accompanied us. We all checked in the same hotel in the morning of the fateful date.

Cheng Peng told us that Nguyen would not meet us in his office. He would inform Cheng Peng at what time and what place he would meet us. After a long wait in suspense, Cheng Peng confirmed the meeting would take place at 8.30 PM in some place.

"Be prepared for an encounter of at least the third kind, if not fourth," I told Rai.

"Hmm..." he muttered with a grim expression. Normally he was very jovial and always free to chat on matters like feminine beauty and adult jokes. For once I found him visibly uncomfortable, at the prospect of being surrounded with a bevy of beautiful girls, in an alien environment. And with the possibility of being trailed by the Vietnamese secret agency.

It was quite dark when we came out of our hotel. Cheng Peng hired a cab. The cab moved through streets and alleys, some of them quite dark. Rai was sitting stiff without muttering a sound.

Finally, the cab stopped in front of a night club. I could see the name of the club shining with bright neon light, which I remember very well even today – 'Club 236'. Though not normally dogmatic about numbers, I have some weakness about numbers that add up to eleven. By some strange coincidence, they generally brought me good luck!

The entry gate was closed with some sturdy uniformed personnel standing there. Cheng Peng told them something in Vietnamese, might be a code word. They immediately opened the gate and let us in.

The lavishly done up lobby was full of beautiful girls in white dresses all around. One of them ushered the three of us into a waiting room which had glass walls all around. As we looked out through the glass walls, only pretty girls in white and some security people in white uniform were visible. Rai, looking quite tense, muttered something unprintable!

Converted to sober and printable English it would mean, "Having an eerie feeling. In spite of seeing so many attractive girls around, I am not getting excited."

After a while a hostess came and led us to 3rd level upstairs along the staircase. At the lobby of each level, there was a security person in white uniform, calling up his counterpart in the upper level for clearance to send us up! Nguyen definitely wanted secrecy!

We were taken to a dining room on the 3rd level. Nguyen was there along with some of his friends being served by a bevy of beautiful girls with drinks. He waved at me as soon as we entered. I was relieved to learn that it was a private party and he wanted a quick meeting.

He asked me specifically to come closer sit next to him, which I did. After a few pleasantries he whispered in my ears some important information.

"The bids have been opened. You are the lowest bidder," he informed.

"The price of Bechtel Corporation, who are the second lowest, is well above yours," he continued. "You are safe. I have already created a document recommending your company to be called for negotiation and finalization of the contract. The paper is being circulated for signatures of all members of our bid evaluation team," he whispered.

"But still remain careful," he added. "The agent of Bechtel has a very strong presence here and may try to derail you. If any query comes to you from our company, please show it to me before sending any reply. Be in touch with me through Cheng Peng."

We spent some time finishing a glass of champagne served by one of the girls.

After a while, I handed over the gift to him, thanked him and bade goodbye.

Sweet Taste of Victory

A few weeks later we got the letter of invitation from Pet-Viet to negotiate and finalize the contract!

We formed a team between Rai, I and our chairman Rudra for the final negotiations. After a few days of detailed negotiations, the contract was signed.

It was the first contract won by Triune in the international environment against bidding and competition from major international players. It was a project of substantial size and value, delivered at the right time when the Hyundai FPSO job was nearing completion in Triune India office.

On my part, it was a vindication of my belief that Triune Singapore could be developed as an outpost for breaking into overseas market.

*****

MALAYSIAN FORAYS

A Business Breakthrough in Malaysia

Malaysia was one of the biggest markets for engineering services in South East Asia. But doing business there without a local representative was very difficult. Someone gave me the contact of Dr. Syed (name changed). A highly qualified management person, he had worked as a senior executive in Petronas, the largest Malaysian energy company and a global player in oil and gas business.

Later, Dr. Syed came out of Petronas and started his own business outfit. A fairly long career in Petronas and with a cordial personality, he had an excellent business network. I had numerous interactions with him. Over a period of time besides being a business associate, he became a close family friend.

Within a short period, Dr. Syed created an opportunity for Triune India to place a multi-disciplinary engineering team of five engineers in Petronas office in Kuala Lumpur, through his company.

I was not very much in favor of this kind of man-power placement. Dr. Syed very clearly explained to me the way to do services business in Malaysia.

"There are only two ways. Malaysia wants engineering services activity to be done from Malaysian soil," he explained. "So, you either place your people with the client company. Or you start a joint venture engineering services company with a local *Bumiputera* (meaning local original inhabitants) as partner here. That joint venture can have a team of your engineers located at their office and can offload some work to your India office. Since at present you don't have a company in

Malaysia, this is the best option to enlarge your network here," he stated.

Setting up a joint venture company in Malaysia was a major effort and investment for which Triune India was not prepared at the time. Triune India went ahead with the opportunity and placed the engineers in Petronas office.

An Ethical Practice

Like most other Asian countries there is graft in Malaysia too. But I call it a well systemized and ethical practice, which does not compromise on quality of work. One of my ex-colleagues from India now settled in Malaysia told me his experience. Here is the story as told by him which exemplifies how it works in Malaysia.

"After arriving in Malaysia, I wanted to get my driving license here. I applied and then was called to appear for a driving test. The official who took my test, did his job very thoroughly making me drive in busy streets for over an hour. Then he told me that I had passed and he would issue the license.

"Then he advised me to apply through a certain agency in Kuala Lumpur. The agency charged some fees and soon I got the license. Obviously, there was some 'arrangement' between the agency and the official.

"But no comprise was made in the quality of testing process by the person."

Similar situations occur in business too.

*****

SINGAPORE MOVES

No Wastage of Time

Amidst the financial and business slump, the opportunities were limited. But on the positive side, everything in Singapore worked as efficiently as before. An American journalist observed that even during financial depression, a streetlight if not working was replaced within hours. Impressed, he wrote an article titled "Singapore Works."

I had already started targeting a second major overseas engineering services order for Triune India. Keeping in line with Triune's new found niche business area, I targeted a prospective FPSO project.

Major international oil and gas companies like Modec and Schlumberger were involved. It called for creating new relationships. Again, the lead for it came from one of my contacts in Singapore.

To fill the gap between, I secured a few small orders direct to our Singapore office.

Also, some orders on the software company of Jacob in India resulted in placement of a few software personnel in our Singapore office. One of the software guys in our office managed to secure an IT related order directly on Triune Singapore.

Our numbers grew to eight. I had some company now; it was a relief from the loneliness!

And a lot more administrative work cropped up. I called one administration person from our Delhi office for support. Sam (name changed), a lively and energetic person from Triune India joined me in Triune Singapore.

Sam had a direct experience of work culture in Singapore on the very second day of his joining. A large payment was due from a client. I called the project manager of the company. He assured me that the cheque would be ready by 2.00 PM. the next day and requested someone to be sent to collect it.

I asked Sam to get the cheque and deposit it in the Triune Singapore bank account.

The next day, Sam went about his mission and returned to our office by 3.30 PM. He gave me his feedback on Singapore's work culture.

"I reached the office of our client ten minutes before 2.00 PM." he said. He continued in an excited tone, "I gave the receptionist my identity and the name of the executive whom I wanted to meet. She called him on the phone and told me that he would be seeing me in a few minutes.

"Within a minute or two, the executive came out at the reception, the cheque in an envelope in his hand. He shook hands with me and asked me to take out the cheque to see that it was in order. I found it okay, thanked him and came out. Depositing it in the bank and coming back to the office using public conveyance hardly took any time."

"No wastage of time anywhere! This is the shortest and quickest official transaction I have done in my life," he concluded, visibly impressed.

A Matter of Business Dynamics

A company can create an overseas office in different modes. It could be *satellite* company replicating the business of the home office in a new location, on its own or by acquisition. Or it could be an overseas *outpost,* normally set up with the objective of a limited activity with minimal staff.

The success of an overseas *outpost* depends a lot on the dynamics of relationship and support from the home office. The support could be in terms of giving lead to expand the network of person-in-charge, regular review interactions with home office and manpower support. A key element is reasonable financial terms for its sustenance, linked to securing orders for home office.

Triune Singapore office was set up as an *outpost* for creating overseas business opportunities for Triune India. My predecessors, Menon and his successor Rajiv, as persons-in-charge of the outpost, brought reasonable benefits to Triune India. There were overseas placements, resulting in improved cash-flow and enlargement of the client base. Also, some work orders on home office materialized, albeit small in size.

Rajiv, added to it by securing some small job orders on Triune Singapore directly.

When I was heading the Triune India office, I used to make visits to Singapore to meet potential clients together with the person in-charge in Singapore office. I used to review business prospects and provide support required by the Singapore office. There was no rigid financial contract between the Singapore office and Delhi office. We used to settle it amicably on case-to-case basis.

But, for quite a few other senior executives in Triune India, the Singapore office was an unnecessary burden. Any lead from the Singapore office, and they would directly visit the client in Singapore, bypassing our Singapore man!

It was an inherent urge to take full credit for securing an order. As an added benefit, eliminate any expenses to be paid to the Singapore office. Such attitude is common in the corporate world.

-----------*A Case Study on Business Dynamics*------------

A senior management person from one of the business outfits of Jacob, visited Triune Singapore in connection with a project. By coincidence, I happened to be present there witnessing an interesting event unfolding.

Our Triune Singapore In-charge completely briefed the executive from India about potential clients and opportunities. Our executive from India was a good listener. He listened in rapt attention.

Once the briefing was over, our executive from India just walked out murmuring something like, "Shall see you later."

He never returned. After meeting the potential clients, he took a flight back to India!

"What is this?" our Singapore man asked me. "He neither asked me to accompany him nor did he brief me about the meetings he had."

"You have to face and manage surprises in life," was my cryptic reply.

THE FINAL EXIT

When I moved to Singapore, I realized how important the dynamics between home office and overseas outpost was.

I had the first experience of business dynamics while negotiating payment receivable from Triune India on the Pet-Viet orders. I felt the tone of negotiation was like an outsider being beaten down on fees for securing the order for Triune India.

A similar lack of empathy and lack of support was noticeable on the second major project from Singapore that landed on Triune India.

A lead to a major offshore FPSO project was given to me by a well-established offshore structural engineering company in Singapore. It was owned and run by an Indian technocrat. The gentleman had become a good friend. He knew the client very well. He helped a lot in getting our capability known to them and get our profiles registered with them.

Though, there was no written or verbal understanding with him, surely, he expected that he would have a role if we got the engineering contract for the project.

After I passed on the lead to Triune India, certain events occurred which gradually took Triune Singapore totally out of the picture.

But I would not fault Triune India management for it. After all they had no stake and no ownership in the performance of Triune Singapore. Their primary interest was to ensure maximum profit and growth for Triune India.

I realized that my style of following the old pattern of relationship between Triune India and Triune Singapore as partner companies, was totally outdated.

At that point, Triune India was well-established in both domestic and overseas markets with lucrative opportunities. My take on this situation was that Triune India management did not find Triune Singapore a necessity for further growth.

It was a debatable conclusion. My point is that we collectively failed to strike proper dynamics between home office and overseas outpost. Individual egos played a spoilsport. I certainly could have tried to change the environment and create an understanding. But by that time destiny was calling me out loud and clear, to make a break and shape my future the way I wanted.

In mid-1999, after the forementioned opportunity turned into an order, I submitted my resignation for my final exit from Triune in the quest of freedom. The freedom I was looking for now was freedom to do what I enjoyed doing and *the freedom of not to do anything I did not enjoy doing*.

I left Triune for good with a great sense of satisfaction. I had given my very best to nurse it from the day it was born in 1990 to a strong adulthood. It had become a well-established and internationally recognized engineering consultancy company.

The vision Jacob and I shared of creating a high-end engineering consultancy company was fulfilled.

It was time to go!

*****

THE AFTERMATH

Jacob was quite upset at my resignation. He was really fond of me and never wanted me to leave Triune so abruptly. Moreover, I resigned a few years ahead of the agreed duration of my stay with Triune Singapore.

There were a few hard exchanges on fax, which I could have avoided by keeping silent. I was sure that he would understand and eventually over a time our relationship would be normal.

I came back to India in the year 2000. Within a few years of my return, our relationship became friendly as before. We started keeping in touch with each other regularly. Sometimes I would drop in at his office and have lunch together updating each other. I would tell him about my activities and he would speak about progress in Triune business in domestic and specifically international arena.

It was circa 2018. One day while having lunch with him, he sprang a surprise for me! He had created something in my name which was like a lifetime award for me! It gave me an immense sense of satisfaction.

What was it? I have touched upon it later in this book.

> *"The beauty of endings
> lies in the fresh starts they bring."*
>
> *-Anonymous*

CHAPTER - 5

FREEDOM! FREEDOM!

EL CÓNDOR PASA

El Cóndor Pasa (The Flight of the Condor) is originally a Peruvian music composed in 1913. More than 4000 versions of it have been produced in the world including one in English in 1970 by Simon and Garfunkel. I specifically enjoyed one of the instrumental versions of it with video. With the lilting music, it was fascinating to see Condor, the majestic bird of the Andes, floating freely high in the sky with its ten-feet wingspan.

When I left Triune Singapore in 1999, it was my final exit from the corporate cobweb. I felt just like the Condor. The original wordings of the song in Spanish (translated in English here) reverberated in my mind...

"The Condor of the Andes wakes anew

With the light, happy and bright, of the dawn..."

At last, I had reached a state where I could always choose what to do.

And choose it keeping in mind, *"When was the last time you did something for the first time."*

To Do What Few Can Do

During my tenure with Triune, I had met an executive in a relatively small sized American company, with business focus on high end of the petroleum refining technology. I met him to probe the possibility of offering engineering services from Triune. In that context I was briefing him about Triune's capabilities and our competitive man-hour costs.

His reply was fascinating to me.

"We occupy a unique position in the high end of the business. We do what not many companies can do. We charge a high price and get it," he replied.

"To us the quality and knowledge base of your people will matter more than the man-hour rates," was his concluding remark.

That statement impressed me. I had decided whatever I do will be focused on what not many could do and at the same time I should enjoy doing it.

And do not let my mind and body retire as long as possible.

The Enterprise Model

We continued to live in Singapore with permanent resident status. My wife Deepali at the time was working with Singapore Environment Council. We both went to the Singapore office of the Registrar of Companies. Systems are so streamlined in Singapore! Within minutes we could register a proprietorship firm with a name of our choice, *Technomanage Consultants*.

We set two objectives of the company- first to provide *Niche Area consultancy services* with the support of a limited number of specialists; and the second was *Corporate Training*.

Niche area consultancy here means kind of knowledge-based services 'what few can do', inspired by the snippet I inserted in just before this section.

Corporate training is a highly competitive market. Here again I had to develop certain unique training programs, which were not commonly offered by others.

One of them, titled *A to Z of Oil & Gas to Petrochemicals*, takes you through the entire chain starting from production of oil and natural gas to fuel filling stations and plastics we use in our daily life. Explained with simple narrative, it became an instant hit.

The other one was a specialist program titled *Developing Basic Design of Process Plants*, specially developed on request from major international consultancy companies.

To create a strong base of professionals, I tied up with experts, mostly my ex-colleagues in India, all experienced professionals on case-to-case basis. To be competitive, we moved back to New Delhi and set up a small but well-equipped office.

Our core team had only four people including myself. There was Rizwan, a young engineer with excellent ability in computer skills related to both hardware and applications software. Deepali looked after marketing, editing and QA/QC. And someone on a part time basis was helping us with our accounts.

It was an easy start-up with the network and credibility we had. All the jobs materialized from contacts in our network, on invited and negotiated basis.

I was taking up jobs selectively, based on what interested me. Yet, a stage of growth came where flow of work orders created excessive work pressure. I had to decide to either call for a pause or do a course change towards a larger corporate outfit.

But before coming to that part of the story, here are some stories and anecdotes of a few exciting and enjoyable experiences.

*****

BUSINESS WITH PLEASURE - ANECDOTES

Facing The Heat from Astute Lawyers

It was an assignment as *Expert Witness* in an arbitration case between a Korean engineering and construction company (turnkey contractor) and a major multinational oil producing company (client). The dispute was over completion of a turnkey contract worth over a billion dollars. There were major disagreements between the two sides on whether the job was technically complete or not. Several hundred million dollars of payments to the Korean contractor were held up by their client. There were major technical and legal issues involved.

I was engaged by the Korean company as an 'Expert Witness' related to conflicts over technical issues. The venue of the arbitration was the London Court of International Arbitration (LCIA).

In any such dispute, there are always issues that do not have straight black and white answers on which side is right or wrong.

The role of the *Expert Witness* is to carry out in-depth study to turn the gray areas into white for his client, based on his technical expertise, experience and logic. And then defend the conclusions under aggressive questioning by astute lawyers.

There were three complex technical issues of different nature to defend. I quickly garnered support from four of my ex-colleagues to help me to analyze the technical issues and prepare the reports for my client.

Then the D-day came to appear before the arbitrators in London to defend my findings!

It was one of the most thrilling experiences, to be grilled by lawyers, under the beautiful setting of London Court of

International Arbitration (LCIA). I reached LCIA a few days ahead of the scheduled date to meet the Korean team and their lawyer, James (name changed).

James, a typical sophisticated British gentleman, impeccably dressed in a dark suit and a crimson tie, had a polished demeanor. But behind that sophistication he displayed a pleasant personality.

He told me how the whole cross examination of the expert witness would be conducted. My cross-examination was on the next day. He advised me to watch the proceedings of cross-examination of one of the witnesses to be ready to face the heat.

"Keep calm and cool," he advised. "Think and then answer, when the opponent's lawyer questions you. Don't lose your cool even under pressure or provocation."

Later, I realized how valuable his advice was!

On the scheduled day of my cross examination, I was taken to the arbitration room by our lawyer. It had a well laid out U-shaped arrangement. The opposing parties faced each other on two sides and the arbitrators at the closed end of the 'U'. In the middle was a chair and a table for the expert witness under the glare of several eyes.

The opposing side's lawyer, another sophisticated personality, got one of my reports opened up on the table in front of me.

He started shooting questions on the report. I noticed that the lawyer was shooting his questions fast.

I realized he did not want to give me any time to think. It was clear that he had studied and understood my technical report thoroughly, despite not having a technical background. He was clearly leading me to the gray areas of my report.

I was replying confidently until he suddenly tore through one of the analyses of my report. He attacked in a firm, polite yet piercing manner, making me fumble for the right answer. Thus, pinning me down, he stated that he had concluded his questioning.

Immediately, our lawyer James took over, seeking permission from the arbitrators to ask me a few questions. He started asking me questions on the same point where I fumbled, but from a different angle and perspective. I realized he was slowly leading me to the right answer to the question where I fumbled.

He ultimately came back exactly to the question where the opposing lawyer had got me fumbling.

This time I could give a firm and confident answer! After the questioning was over, I came out of the witness box highly impressed with the understanding and acumen of our lawyer. I thanked him and he patted me with a smiling face.

I really enjoyed the interaction with two suave lawyers. My respect for lawyers went up!

*****

TRAINING TOO CAN BE FUN – ANECDOTES

I started with delivering open training programs for industries in the South East Asia, under the banner of National University of Singapore (NUS). Executives from many countries in the region participated in the programs. By word of mouth from the participants, its popularity spread around the world. I had to do quite a bit of traveling with my team.

Here are some snippets of interesting incidents during our training forays.

Invitation for a World Tour

We were delivering an open program on "A to Z of Oil & Gas to Petrochemicals" in Singapore, with executives from numerous industries participating. On the last day after conclusion of the program, I saw an American gentleman participating in the program coming down the steps of the lecture theater. He shook hands with me. I waited in anticipation to hear him.

"I am Director Engineering in Solar Turbines, USA," he said after introducing with his name.

"I liked your program. Would you like to deliver your program in our offices in Singapore, San Diego, Houston (USA) and our European locations?" He asked.

Who would say "no" to such an offer!

Obviously, I happily replied in the affirmative. It resulted in a series of lectures around the world.

The Thai Female Companion

The setting of this story was in the southern part of Thailand in the training centre of Petroleum Authority of Thailand. We were there to conduct a 15-day training program on Natural Gas

Processing. I had a strong team of four experts with me and Deepali as editor and coordinator.

At the start of the program, I introduced each member of the team. Then I started presentation of the technical slides. But for the first time in my several programs worldwide, looking at the eyes of the audience, I felt that something was amiss.

I felt that I was not communicating well enough. I realized that the Thai participants were not so well conversant with English. And to add to that, the difference in the accents! I had a creepy feeling that whatever I presented was going over their head. I slowed down my delivery and somewhat established communication and rapport.

Later, I realized my initial introduction of team members had failed to register with them. During lunch break, one official of the Thai management team sat down with us. While eating and chatting, he threw a bombshell of a question.

"Is the lady with you, your Thai female companion?" He asked.

Taken aback, I wondered whether to respond in the affirmative, for fun. Coming from the north-eastern part of India closer to Thailand, Deepali has streaks of South-east Asian features and petite look. But I decided that on such an official event, that kind of joke would not go well. Smilingly, I disclosed her identity.

The gentleman was apologetic and complemented her by saying that she looked like a beautiful Thai girl.

---------------------------**Incidentally**---------------------------

My 'Thai female companion' did a commendable job in managing one hostile member of the client's management team. A knowledgeable person in natural gas processing technology, he had planned to conduct the training of his people himself, without going to an outside agency. Management had overruled him.

He certainly acted as if he was unhappy about our presence. He was interrupting us at every opportunity, explaining things to the participants in Thai language, incomprehensible to us.

After such interventions, Deepali took an interesting initiative. At lunch break, I saw her joining the gentleman for lunch in a separate table and having a friendly conversation.

Wisely, I took a table quite away from them. I did not know what conversation she had with him, but the effect was miraculous. From then onwards, there was no interference and he became very polite and cooperative. I later enquired how she had that magical effect on the Thai gentleman.

"It was empathy," Deepali replied.

In her diverse career, she had worked as a teacher in a high school. She just expressed her appreciation to him as a teacher, for his zeal to ensure that the trainees got the best out of the program. She also told him that we were aware that there was a communication gap and assured that our team would make sure that the gap is closed. That established an immediate rapport.

The Healing Effect of an Audience

It was circa 2006. Deepali and I reached Brussels to conduct a training program at the European Center of a major multinational.

During our journey from Delhi, I developed some health issues. I had taken some snacks at the stop-over at Amsterdam, to which my stomach totally disagreed and revolted. When we reached our hotel in Brussels in the evening, I was feeling giddy, had nausea. I immediately lied down in the bed in the hotel room. Soon I started throwing up everything I had eaten. I was feeling sick and was wondering how I would deliver the two-day program starting at 9.00 AM the next morning. I took some emergency medicines which we always carry.

The medicines gave some relief. After I got up in the morning, I was feeling weak. But I felt that I could deliver my program.

As I entered the training center, it was bustling with participants. Just looking at the gathering, coming from all over Europe, waiting to hear me had a magical healing effect. Within minutes I started feeling better. Something inside started recharging me!

By the time I took the podium, I felt full of vigor and energy!

*****

THE TURNING POINT

Take a Break

"Keep your brain ticking as you grow older," was the advice from some celebrity in his early nineties to his son, a scientist, closing in on seventies.

That exactly was one of the major objectives of creating Technomanage Consultants.

For the first decade (till 2010) after starting Technomanage Consultants, I was maintaining a balance between work, life and enjoyment. But somehow our name spread by word of mouth.

At one point after 2010, the flow of enquiries, particularly for consultancy, became excessive. Even after responding selectively, job orders were turning into burden for our small outfit, affecting our quality of life. Though I must admit, this was the period which made us financially strong for a comfortable future.

We had started as a proprietorship firm with no intention to create another company. For once, I seriously pondered whether we should create one.

But wiser sense prevailed. Deepali and I felt a need to decelerate the pace of life.

In 2011, we dropped consultancy work almost totally from our agenda and *wisely* kept only training as our professional activity. I used the word *wisely* because focusing on training alone, made a dramatic improvement in the quality of life and work-life balance.

Firstly, it satisfied my intense urge inside to interact with the younger generation and pass on to them what I have learnt.

Add to that the fun of taking a break in between different training assignments. To give an example, after completing a training program in Belgium, Deepali and I decided to take a break to spend some memorable time in Vienna and Salzburg, historic towns with unique charm.

Around 2017, frequent traveling on corporate training was getting too much. I decided to opt out of onsite or classroom type of corporate training.

*****

SOMETHING NEW AGAIN

Every end can be turned into the start of some new beginning!

I am now in the process of making our training programs available online. It has been a new and exciting learning process.

Our daughter and son-in-law, both IT specialists, helped in creating the website for online learning (technomanage.com) and helped me select a special software for conversion of my power point slides to online format with narration.

Frankly I found my task quite daunting! Opening the slides in my laptop and speaking to a ghost audience to record the narrative was really a tough task. The flow of words used to come naturally to me while interacting with a live audience.

On online format, I have nobody in front of me to interact. And no second chance to clarify immediately to any question the audience might have!

I realized that for every slide I have to write a script, speak in a slow and clear voice for recording, and synchronize with the animation on the slide. Then listen to it, revise and edit. It was like making a movie, shot by shot!

It took a long time and effort.

At the time of writing this memoir, I have completed some of my training programs online and uploaded them at the website. I hope the work will lead to the benefit of many.

But then what next? Another beginning?

AFTERWORD

That was the story of the journey of an ordinary person through the corporate cobweb. It has been a satisfying, thrilling and enjoyable journey. One of the most rewarding things in life has been the greetings I continue to receive from many of my juniors who worked with me and became very successful in life – some of them in business, some in top management echelons. Some of them send me greetings on Teachers' Day every year acknowledging my contribution to their success.

Something for me to remember for a lifetime came from Jacob!

It was circa 2018. I got a call from Jacob, he asked me to join him for lunch in Triune office in New Delhi. As usual we met and started chatting. He shared with me about a major new project on offshore oil production awarded to Triune. He described some major revamp done in the Triune office in order to meet certain requirements of the client.

"I have added a few new conference rooms," he said. Then he started telling me the names, he has given to the new conference rooms, one by one.

The first two were named after some floating oil production systems engineered by Triune. The name of the third room that he announced was unexpected but a pleasant surprise for me!

"The third meeting room...," he gave a brief pause and continued, "has been named *'UKD Room'* in remembrance of you." To avoid any confusion for the reader, UKD stands for initials of my full name.

I was deeply moved by the gesture and thanked him. I left Triune in India in 1997 and Triune Singapore in 1999. It was a great gesture of honor that a company would remember my contribution 20 years after my exit and keep a permanent symbol in their office!

At the end of my first chapter regarding my exit from Engineers India Limited, I had mentioned a quote-

"When you leave a place you love, a part of it remains with you and a part of you remains there." I got the same kind of feeling with Jacob's gesture.

A part of Triune has always remained with me. It was an exhilarating feeling to see that a part of me would continue to live with Triune.

Frankly, I never thought I did anything more than completing a responsibility that I took up. Quite a few others besides Jacob, the owner, contributed enormously in shaping Triune. On my mentioning this, I received interesting response Jacob.

In his usual style he wrote to me, "It is one of the greatest successes in your life. I say that because a Start-Up/ Entrepreneurial pursuit has the lowest probability of success among all the professional options one pursues. In everything else you did, the risks were lower, you were better qualified to succeed, the chances of success were much higher. Today, Triune is known the world over in the Oil Industry because of you."

"...Many luminaries passed through Triune portal and made extraordinary contributions. But you made that portal, and your contribution was the most valuable." He added.

Jacob is a person who always talks straight on what he genuinely believes, without mincing any words. His last statement made me feel that I must have done something good.

The foreword of this book titled 'The Curtain Raiser' starts with a quote, *"When was the last time you did something for the first time?"* I continue my life with the same spirit within the limits imposed by the passage of time. Now I have taken to writing. Writing books, both technical and non-technical, and creating my own blog sites, based on my experiences on various aspects of life.

My first publication titled "Hop Stop & Go, Fascinating Encounters..." was based on interactions with different cultures during my travels around the world. It received some excellent reviews from readers.

A very satisfying comment from one of readers of Hop Stop & Go was, *"This book has inspired my son who loves learning about cultures of different countries, to write about his own travel experiences."*

This kind of impact on a teenager gives immense satisfaction to an author. It will be equally satisfying if this book also inspires some greenhorn of young age to start-up his own company.

I love to conclude with my favorite quote from a poem by Robert Frost...

[Courtesy: Deepali Dutta]

"Miles to go before I sleep"

POSTSCRIPT

When the book was about to be published, an unforeseen tragic event occurred, necessitating addition of this postscript. Jacob, one of the of the main characters of my book passed away on January 18, 2024.

Certain cells in Jacob's body had revolted. He had developed cancer. A fighter that he was, we had hopes that he would win this battle also. A month or so before his death, I with my wife Deepali had met him in his home. He was weak, lying in bed. But his voice was strong. When we were about to leave, he got up and looked at me. I saw a lot of strength in his eyes, raising my hopes that he would be able to fight it out.

But that was not to be. Providence took away our friend.

We shall miss you Binoy Jacob. Rest in peace! Amen!

www.ingramcontent.com/pod-product-compliance
Lightning Source LLC
Chambersburg PA
CBHW020424010526
44118CB00010B/417